FLOWER GARDENING FOR BEGINNERS

FLOWER GARDENING
for Beginners

A Guide to Growing and Maintaining a Cut Flower Garden

Amy Barene
Illustrations by Liam O'Farrell

ROCKRIDGE PRESS

First Rockridge Press trade paperback edition 2022

Rockridge Press and the Rockridge Press logo are trademarks or registered trademarks of Callisto Media Inc. and/or its affiliates in the United States and other countries and may not be used without written permission.

For general information on our other products and services, please contact our Customer Care Department within the United States at (866) 744-2665, or outside the United States at (510) 253-0500.

Paperback ISBN: 978-1-68539-105-8
eBook ISBN: 978-1-68539-987-0

Manufactured in the United States of America

Interior and Cover Designer: Linda Kocur
Art Producer: Samantha Ulban
Editor: Van Van Cleave
Production Editor: Rachel Taenzler
Production Manager: Lanore Coloprisco

Illustrations © 2022 Liam O'Farrell. All photography used under license © Shutterstock. Author photo courtesy of Leesha King Photography.

10 9 8 7 6 5 4 3 2 1 0

To my grandma:
My perfect day would be spent
having tea with you in a garden.

PEONY [page 94]

Contents

PART 1: Flower Gardening Basics

PART 2: Flower Profiles

Introduction

When I was younger, my mom used to place a small jar of fresh-cut flowers in my room. They weren't anything fancy: a few roses, stems of rosemary, and a couple of small flowering bits. I watched her do this whenever we had company, or when I came home from college. It was a small, sweet way to show she cared. I imagine that, like me, you hold a special place in your memories for cut flowers. There is something so touching knowing that someone has tended and cut their garden blooms just for you to enjoy. Having been on both the receiving and growing end of cut flowers, I can assure you that the joy as the grower is tenfold greater.

My fascination with plants and flowers started in my grandmother's and mother's gardens, but it wasn't until my adult years that growing my own became my passion. As a child, weeding was a chore—why would I want to do it for fun? However, after graduating college, I found myself teaching at a school with a garden. And not just any garden—this garden had hundreds of plants, including my personal favorite, dahlias. Soon I was out in the garden during my lunch breaks, before and after school, and even on my summer vacation. After the first season, I took home twenty tubers (the root stock of dahlia plants) and planted them in my first raised bed.

That year, with only twenty plants and no experience, I grew a bounty of blooms that I proudly gifted to friends, neighbors, and family. Over the years, that one garden bed grew into half my yard, and my small cut flower bouquets evolved into a full business. Now my husband and I grow and sell flowers for weddings, florists, music videos, and art installations.

All this began with a simple dream: to go out to my garden and put together a whimsical, garden-fresh bouquet to brighten my home and those of my loved ones. If you're reading this book, maybe you have a similar dream. Maybe you've even tried growing a flower garden before, but it just never worked out. With this book, it is my aim to help make that dream a reality for you. I will walk you through the basics of starting a garden, maintaining it, harvesting your flowers, and arranging your grown blooms.

In part 1, we'll dive into the foundational elements of gardening. In these chapters, we will investigate where your garden would best thrive in your yard, how your local climate affects your plants, and how you can build your own garden beds. Once we have set your garden up for success, we'll dive into the fun part—picking out seeds and plants. I'll share my tips on how to select seeds that will be successful in your garden and how to best plant and care for them. Note that although I started my cut flower garden with just one flower variety, there are dozens of beginner flower varieties that are accessible for first-time gardeners, thirty-five of which I will profile in part 2 of this book. These profiles will detail how to start flowers from seed, how to harvest them, and how best to display them, so that you can grow your own favorite flowers year after year.

Above all, my hope is that by the end of this book, you will have discovered some blooms that you love and will feel empowered to grow them yourself. I can envision you, too, headed out into your yard, eager to see what new flowers have blossomed, and creating special bouquets for yourself and your loved ones. I hope you will feel the same sense of curiosity and joy at the beauty of your very own cut flower garden and that you will fully enjoy the fruits of your labor. I promise that the process of gardening will reward you with experiences even more special than the flowers you harvest.

How to Use This Book

If you've picked up this book, I imagine you are feeling the way I did when I bought my first seeds: eager and excited, but with no clue where to start. Fortunately, this book will meet you where you're at! This comprehensive guide contains everything you'll need to know in order to plan, grow, tend, and harvest your cut flower garden. The chapters are laid out sequentially, starting with the very basics and continuing to profiles of specific flowers to choose from. To build on your gardening knowledge as you progress through the chapters, the book is divided into the following two parts:

Part 1: Flower Gardening Basics

In part 1, we will go over the essential elements of starting your cut flower garden. Here we'll address questions like "Where in my yard should I start my garden?", "How do I build a raised bed?", "What kind of soil do I need?", and "What will grow best in my climate?" We'll also dive into specific gardening tools and terms that will equip you for long-term success as a gardener. In these chapters, you will also find visual aids and tables, like an example garden journal entry (page 11), that will serve as handy references even after you've finished reading this book. Finally, we'll dive into the basics of arranging cut flowers so that you can put your beautiful blooms to use.

Part 2: Flower Profiles

In part 2, you get to focus on selecting which blooms you want to grow. You'll find thirty-five flower profiles, organized by their growing seasons. Each profile provides a clear and in-depth look at how each plant grows, produces, and thrives. These specific flowers are all accessible for beginner growers and were chosen for their versatility and high growing potential as cut flowers.

Additionally, in each flower profile, you will find a quick reference box, tips, and details about how to grow and care for each cut flower plant. Think of these profiles as your simple road map to take you from seed germination to flower preservation!

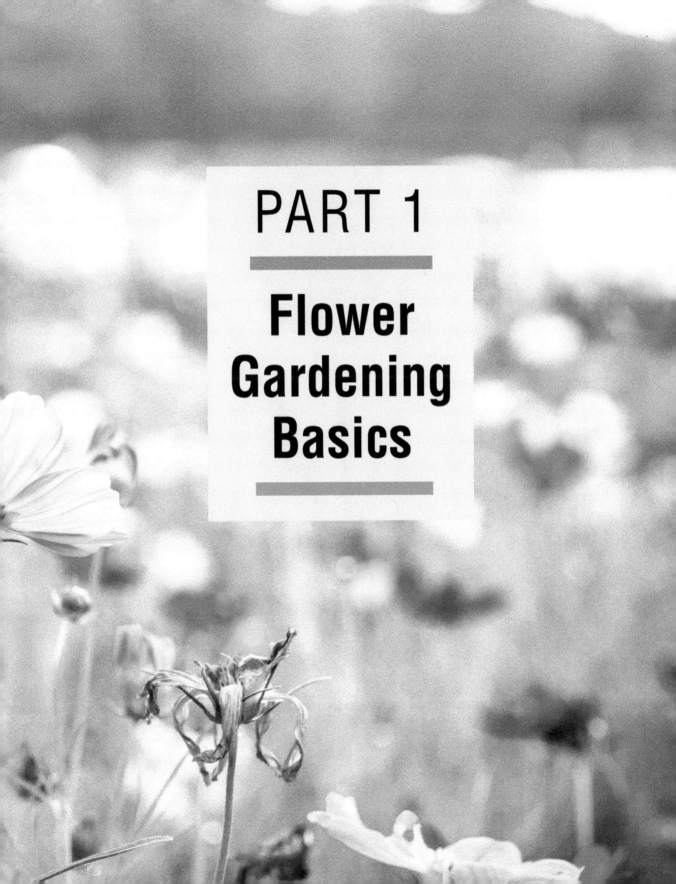

PART 1

Flower Gardening Basics

TULIP [page 102]

1

Getting Started

Let's be honest: We've all killed plants before. They were overwatered, underwatered, dried up, or simply forgotten. However, most of these casualties stem from skipping over one essential step: setting up your garden for success. Although it is tempting to rush out and buy seeds or plants before planning where they will go or knowing what they need, we need to lay the proper groundwork first. In this chapter, we will cover why you should grow cut flowers in the first place and how to do so successfully by discussing common gardening terms, tools, and techniques. Read through this chapter carefully to establish your foundation as a cut flower gardener.

Why Grow Your Own Flowers?

If you've chosen to start your cut flower garden journey, you are probably a fellow flower lover. Maybe you enjoy buying bouquets at your weekend farmers' market, like I do, or can't resist picking up some blooms at the grocery store. Maybe you are interested in making arrangements for your loved ones. Or perhaps you're a florist looking to grow your own blossoms for your business. Regardless, there are many benefits to growing and harvesting your own flowers.

Few things add beauty to your home and yard like fresh flowers. Indoors and out, they add color and freshness to brighten any space, and they can even impact your well-being. In fact, after gardening for multiple years, I saw an improvement in my mental health. Not just from the flowers (although that played a big part in it!), but from getting outside, moving my body, and breathing fresh air. Gardening quickly became one of my favorite parts of the day.

Growing your own flowers also has a positive impact on the environment. The imported flowers we find in grocery stores are typically wrapped in plastic and contain chemical additives that put undue stress on our environment. By planting your own garden, you are not only eliminating your purchases of imported flowers; you are also adding oxygen back into the air, which in turn improves air quality.

Lastly, starting a flower garden creates a place for pollinators to thrive. Flowers encourage the presence of natural pollinators such as bees, butterflies, and hummingbirds, which helps keep the balance of a healthy ecosystem. Though we start our gardens for different reasons, we can all share in the happiness and health that a garden provides.

7 Things to Know Before You Grow

As you start to plan your garden, it's worth keeping a few guiding principles in mind. Let these seven tips be your gardening tenets before you dig in.

Location is key. Choosing the right location for your garden is the first step in setting it up for success. This is because different plants have different sunlight and water needs and can be impacted by natural elements like wind and ground incline. We will discuss how to choose the perfect location for your garden in chapter 2.

Not all dirt is created equal. Don't expect your soil to be ready to go when you dig into the ground. Depending on your climate and what flowers you are growing, different soils and additives will be necessary for lush, happy plants. Some natural soils have heavy sand deposits, some are full of clay, and some are nutrient deficient. We'll dive into soil in chapter 3.

Grow to your climate. Not every plant flourishes in every environment. When picking out what cut flowers you are going to grow, make sure that you can give the plants the light, temperature, and moisture that they require. Also keep in mind that not all flowers will last through all seasons. In February, what might be blooming in California would be covered in snow in the Midwest. In chapter 2, you'll learn how to determine your unique climate and growing seasons.

Be patient. Not every flower blooms during its first season, and not every seed germinates within its expected window. Some flowers are an investment in that they may produce few to no blooms during their first growing season. Be patient with perennials and know that in the long run, you will be rewarded with beautiful blooms.

Don't be afraid to try again. Sometimes you may have to try a few times to get a flower to germinate or grow. Plants can be finicky—if there is something that you would love to have in your garden and for some reason it just keeps not working out, don't be afraid to keep trying! Experiment with different watering schedules, planting locations, and seed-sowing tricks to find what works. Nothing is a better teacher than experience.

You're going to kill some flowers. This is the best advice I've ever gotten as a gardener. It's inevitable that not all your seeds will blossom. That's nature. Once I understood this, it took the pressure off me to make sure everything bloomed every single season.

Take it easy and take it slow. Start with where you are now. You don't need to invest a lot of time and money into growing a cut flower garden; some simple tools, seeds, and soil are all you need to get started. Knowing the basic principles of gardening will provide you with a solid foundation that can be expanded upon every season. Focus on a few beginner varieties to plant and enjoy the process!

Common Gardening Terms

This book is written to be easily understood by beginner gardeners, and therefore avoids using advanced agricultural jargon. However, there are a few basic garden terms that will help anyone reading this book understand it better. Read on to develop your gardening lingo.

Annual: A plant that completes its life cycle in one growing season

Biannual: A plant that blooms twice in a year

Biennial: A plant that puts off leaves the first season and flowers the second season before completing its life cycle

Bulb: The resting stage of flowers, such as tulips, that grows after planting

Compost: A mixture of decaying natural matter used to fertilize plants

Corm: The underground stem base that is the starting form of many spring flowers

Cut and come again: Describes flowering plants that continue to produce blooms after being cut

Days to maturity: The average number of days from germination to first bloom

Deadheading: Cutting dead flowers off to encourage new growth

Direct sow: Planting seeds directly into the soil outdoors

Dividing: Cutting or separating the new growth on a root system to create more plants

Fertilizer: A natural or chemical mixture that improves the soil's nutrients

Full sun: Receiving at least six hours of sunlight, as a garden location

Germination: The stage at which a seed begins to sprout after being dormant

Hardening off: Exposing a plant to a colder environment to acclimate it before planting

Hardiness zone: A set area defined by its average annual temperature range

Last/first frost date: The average dates when an area experiences freezing temperatures

Leggy: Having a long plant stem and sparse leaves due to lack of light

Part sun/part shade: Receiving between four and six hours of sunlight, as a garden location

Perennial: A plant that comes back for multiple growing seasons

Pinching: Cutting a plant at an early stage to encourage growth

Raised bed: A garden bed built above the ground with added soil

Soil amendment: Anything added to soil to improve its physical condition

Starts: Strong seedlings that have been acclimated to the outdoors

Thinning: Removing extra seedlings to prevent crowded plants

Transplanting: Planting a seedling started indoors outside or moving a plant from one place to another

Tuber: The rootstock of dahlia plants

Essential Flower Gardening Tools

Gardening is an accessible and rewarding hobby for all. You don't need new, expensive tools to get started. Here you'll find a list of the basic tools that every type of home gardener needs. We'll go into specific materials for raised beds and containers later in chapter 3.

Gloves: Gloves are an essential tool to protect your hands from splinters and thorns. Select gloves that are machine washable and have palm-dipped coating. I use the brand SHOWA.

Gardening scissors: For the delicate precision of flower gardening, I prefer gardening scissors to shears. Bonsai scissors are a favorite because they are sharp and nimble.

Garden fork: Gardening forks are key for digging up tubers and root structures because they cause less damage to plants than shovels. They are also great for digging up weeds.

Garden hoe/shovel: Hoes and shovels are used to move and mix soil. Hoes can be especially helpful when creating rows to sow seeds.

Seed-starting containers: When starting seeds indoors, use seed containers and leakproof trays to separate seedlings and to bottom water during a plant's early stages. I like the ones from Johnny's Selected Seeds.

Grow light: For some plants, the light from a windowsill is not enough. LED shop lights from your local hardware store provide full-coverage light to help your plants grow.

Hand trowel: Hand trowels are the perfect tool for planting individual seedlings in your garden or weeding throughout the season. The Ames brand gel grip model is a favorite of mine.

Hose with adjustable nozzle: A reliable hose with an adjustable nozzle will aid in easy watering of many different plant varieties. Look for one with a "shower" setting.

Twine: A garden basic, twine is essential for corralling growing flower beds and tying up climbing flowers, such as sweet peas. Bonus: natural twine is biodegradable!

Wheelbarrow: For moving dirt and garden materials, there's nothing better. Choose a fully plastic wheelbarrow— sometimes referred to as a "garden cart"—to prevent weathering.

8 Beginner Steps to a Successful Flower Garden

Now that you're excited to start your garden, let's go over a few practical steps you can follow while planning what to include.

Start small so you don't get overwhelmed. You can grow a large volume of flowers from even the smallest spaces! Two or three beds will provide you with buckets of blooms during the harvesting season. Start with just a few varieties, and then expand your garden once you feel comfortable.

Know your space and be realistic about what will grow in it. The best plants to grow are the ones that will flourish in your unique space. For example, if you do not have sunlight access during the day to grow a certain flower, the plant will not thrive like you would hope. Know your climate (more on that in chapter 2) and take note of what flowers you see in gardens in your neighborhood, as they are good indicators for what might work for you.

Build in time to regularly upkeep your garden. Staying on top of weeding and garden maintenance will ensure that your cut flowers are happy. Pick a time of the day to spend in your garden and add it to your calendar. I like to garden right after work; I can dedicate a good amount of time to upkeep, and it helps me decompress.

Keep to a schedule. Plants love a routine, especially when it comes to watering. Keeping to a regular watering schedule will ensure that your plants hydrate at the optimal time of day. To make it even easier, basic watering drip line kits can be installed in your garden. You can program them for your watering schedule, and they'll do the work for you (see page 59).

You don't have to do it all in one season. When you're a gardener, there is always something more to be done. With growing, tending, harvesting, and saving, your to-do list can feel endless. Know that there are steps you do not need to complete in your first growing season. If saving the seeds of your flowers doesn't happen, don't sweat it! If you decide not to dig up your dahlias the first year, that's totally okay.

Your garden is year-round, even if the blooms aren't. Expanding on the last point, gardening doesn't just happen in the summer. Often December is my only month off from doing something garden-related. With planning in the new year, starting seeds in February and March, planting out in spring, harvesting in summer, and cleaning up in fall, your new hobby is a year-round venture!

Plant with a plan. As we will illustrate in chapter 2, planting with spacing and your surroundings in mind is key. Not all flowers do well when planted together, and plants need to be given adequate room to grow. What starts out as a small seedling will grow wider and taller in time. Make sure to plan for appropriate growing mates and growing space (see page 18).

Cut flowers need to be cut. You've grown a garden for cut flowers, so be sure to spend the time cutting them! Many of the cut flower varieties in this book benefit from being cut regularly. Plan to harvest your blooms as soon as they make an appearance. Don't worry; it's so rewarding to cut what you've grown that this step is far from a chore.

Keeping a Gardening Journal

One of the most important things you can do if you want to have a successful and thriving garden year after year is to keep a gardening journal! A journal allows you to keep all your garden information in one place to easily reference throughout the growing season. Although there are digital and preprinted garden journals available, a classic notebook does the job. Read on for more information on what specifically to include in your journal, and see the image on page 11 for an example of what your journal might look like.

What you are growing. Your journal is a perfect place to document what you are wanting to grow and where you plan to get seeds. You can also keep a wish list of what you hope to grow in the future!

When you should plant. Somewhere in your journal, you will want to keep a calendar of your planting times. A cumulative calendar—documenting everything you are growing and when it should be started indoors, directly sown, or transplanted outside—is a handy tool for reviewing the big picture at a glance.

Plant details. Every flower has different needs. For example, some plants are started indoors, whereas others are not, and some need to be germinated with light and others don't. I recommend dedicating a page or two to each plant to document the details of every flower you have chosen. In order to keep your plant details handy, one trick is to tape or paste your empty seed packets directly into your journal.

Garden layout. One of the first things I add to my garden journal every season is my garden layout plan. I like to sketch out my yard, including where I plan to put my garden beds and what I aim to grow in them. As every flower has its own spacing needs, a garden plan is a perfect way to sketch out how many plants of each flower can fit comfortably in a bed. To easily picture your proportions, try drawing your beds with 1 inch representing 1 foot.

Keeping notes. Unfortunately, not everything will grow as well as you hoped. In your journal, plan to keep some basic notes about how your plants performed as cut flowers. For example, maybe the stems turned out to be short and difficult to work with—make a note to remind yourself not to grow that variety in the future or to try a new method. This will help you better your practice, season after season.

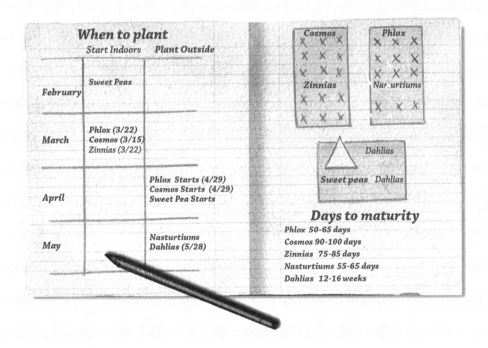

When to plant

	Start Indoors	Plant Outside
February	Sweet Peas	
March	Phlox (3/22) Cosmos (3/15) Zinnias (3/22)	
April		Phlox Starts (4/29) Cosmos Starts (4/29) Sweet Pea Starts
May		Nasturtiums Dahlias (5/28)

Cosmos   Phlox

Zinnias   Nasturtiums

Dahlias

Sweet peas   Dahlias

Days to maturity

Phlox 50-65 days
Cosmos 90-100 days
Zinnias 75-85 days
Nasturtiums 55-65 days
Dahlias 12-16 weeks

FAQ: First-Time Flower Gardeners

Over the years, I've received a lot of questions about cut flower gardening. Let's go over a few common FAQs here.

Q: What is the difference between a cut flower garden and a regular flower garden?

> **A:** As the name suggests, a cut flower garden consists of flowers that are intended to be cut for display or arrangement purposes. For example, flowers like petunias or pansies are beautiful blooms that are often used in landscaping but, due to their short stems, they don't make good cut flowers. The flowers referenced in this book are all tried-and-true varieties that produce ample flowers with long stems intended to be cut and enjoyed. Cut flowers also differ slightly from landscaping blooms as they usually benefit from being cut throughout the season. A cut flower garden is one that you can go out and harvest daily in peak season!

Q: Why should I grow flowers instead of vegetables?

> **A:** There is no need to choose! In fact, flowers are a wonderful addition to a vegetable garden because of their ability to attract pollinators. Bees, butterflies, and hummingbirds are all attracted to the bright colors of flowers and will pollinate both your flowers and vegetables. Having flowers in a vegetable garden will lead to healthier, fuller plants and a thriving ecosystem. If you are looking to start a vegetable garden at the same time as your cut flower garden, *Vegetable Gardening for Beginners* by Jill McSheehy is a great place to start.

Q: What kind of garden should I build?

> **A:** There are many different types of spaces where you can grow your garden. Raised beds, containers, and rows are all common ways to plant. What type of garden is right for you depends on the space you have and what your goals are. Read chapter 3 for more information on how to choose the best garden type for you.

Q: What should I plant?

A: Since we are planting a cut flower garden, growing things with the end product in mind is a good place to start. What do you want in your arrangement? What are your favorite colors? What flowers last a long time in a vase? When picking out your garden blooms, try to plant different shapes and textures. By planting flowers that are different but complementary, you'll have stunning arrangements during your flowering season. In a typical arrangement, you'll want something that can act as a round focal flower (like a dahlia or zinnia), something spiky (like a snapdragon), and filler flowers, such as phlox or cosmos, to add texture. Plant accordingly!

Q: Why haven't my seeds grown in the past?

A: There can be a lot of reasons why seeds haven't grown. One of the most common reasons is that the seeds are of poor quality. Seeds should be purchased from a reputable seed company or directly from the farm. Seeds from big-box retailers are often stored incorrectly and for too long, resulting in low germination rates. Another reason your seeds may not have sprouted is due to their germination requirements. Some plants need light, and others don't; some need it warm, and others don't. We'll go over how to care for each type of seed in chapter 4.

HYACINTH [page 192]

2

Planning Your Flower Garden

Before you place your first seed order, let's come up with a plan for your garden. Understanding your environment and weather patterns will help you choose the flowers best suited for your garden and ensure a lush, thriving flower patch. In this chapter, we will examine your local climate, determine your growing zone, and provide tips for choosing the right flowers accordingly.

Understanding Your Local Climate

Sunlight and temperature are two key ingredients in gardening successfully. Every region has its own weather, and every plant has its own sun and water needs. To that end, where you live will inform what you can grow. Play to your region's strengths and you'll have a beautiful, bountiful cutting garden!

Determine Your Growing Zone

First things first: Figuring out your regional growing zone will help guide you to choose the plants that are likely to thrive in your garden. There are 13 plant hardiness zones that make up the growing zone map. These zones are determined by an area's average minimum winter temperature, and the zones are separated by ten degrees Fahrenheit. The zone numbers are then divided again into subcategories of "A" and "B," which represent a five-degree difference. Zones 1 through 5 grow cold-hardy plants successfully, whereas zones 10 through 13 can often grow flowers year-round due to their warmer winters. Zones 6 through 9 are usually more temperate and make up the large majority of hardiness zones. To find your hardiness zone, you can visit the United States Department of Agriculture's hardiness zones map online or check the Zone Map in the back of this book (see page 159).

Figure Out Your Growing Season

After you figure out your growing zone, you're ready to figure out your growing season. This is one of the most important parts of planting outdoors, no matter the size, shape, or type of garden you're growing. The first thing to know is your average frost dates, or the dates when your region typically gets its first frost of the season in the fall and its last frost of the season in the spring. These dates can then help you determine your growing season, or when you can plant your flowers. Most plants, especially seedlings, are not frost-tolerant, so they must be planted at the right time and temperature. To find your frost dates, you can visit The Old Farmer's Almanac website at Almanac.com.

Staying on Top of Your Growing Climate

In addition to knowing your growing zone, it is a good idea to keep track of your microclimate. I also recommend revisiting your growing zone map and keeping track of climate change and temperature patterns every season or so. This will help you determine what you can and can't grow during a particular time frame. Some useful resources on how changing climates affect flower growing include the plant zone finder tools on Gurneys.com/zone_finder and the hardiness zones plant lists on Gardenia.net.

Where Should You Put Your Flower Garden?

As mentioned previously, the location of your garden within your yard matters a lot because it informs what you can grow there, especially as it relates to a plant's needs for sunlight. Naturally, it is difficult to change your garden's location in the middle of growing, so I recommend taking the following considerations seriously *before* you plant.

Follow the Sun

Observing which parts of your yard get sunlight and shade and recording how much of each is key to knowing what flowers you can grow. Some plants need at least six hours of sunlight daily (full sun), and therefore need access to more direct light, whereas some flourish in the shade and need very little direct sunlight (partial sun). If flowers are not planted with their correct light needs in mind, they could end up leggy (see page 7) with not enough sunlight or burn with too much sunlight.

Site It within Sight

When it comes to gardening, the phrase "out of sight, out of mind" is very applicable. It's easy to forget to tend to your garden if you're not seeing it regularly! To that end, I recommend establishing your garden in a place that you see frequently and have easy access to. This will allow you to successfully manage your garden year-round.

Access to Water (But Not Too Much)

When planning where your garden will be, consider your access to water. Planting your garden close to a water spigot will allow for easy watering—you won't have to carry a watering can back and forth over to your flowers. Be sure to also know where your gutter drains and where the low points of your yard are. You don't want to build your garden in a location that is prone to flooding or standing water.

Planning for Year-Round Blooms

Have you ever noticed that some gardens seem to always be in bloom? Gardeners do this by planting a variety of flowers that develop seasonally throughout the year. To design a year-round flower bed, find a portion of your garden that caters to many different varieties of plants. Focusing on perennials, colorful foliage, and regionally native flowers will ensure that your garden has happy plants that provide cut flowers year after year. Even in the colder zones, gardeners can find frost-hardy plants, such as hellebores, to diversify their garden beds and add pops of color in the cooler months.

Pick Plants That Get Along

In some cases, you can choose to grow plants in close proximity that mutually benefit one another. In the gardening world, this is much more prevalent in vegetable gardening than in flower gardening. However, there are some things to keep in mind when picking flowering plant companions.

Most important, take into account the full-grown size and natural environmental needs of the plants you plant next to one another. Flowers in the same bed will need to share the same light and watering requirements to coexist. Also, keep the height of your plants similar in order to ensure they all get equal access to sunlight. For example, it would not be wise to plant cosmos next to pansies, because cosmos get bushy and tall, therefore blocking out the sunlight needed by the shorter pansies.

There is some evidence to suggest that certain flowers aid in keeping pests at bay for other plants. For example, planting marigolds near sweet peas is said to help prevent aphid infestations. However, in my experience, this is not effective enough to take it as a steadfast rule. Planning your flower bed's companion mates based on space, sun, water, and soil requirements is the most effective way to ensure they will coexist and thrive.

FAQ: A Flower Gardener's First Steps

As you're planning your garden, you may have some questions. Here are some quick responses to five common ones.

Q: What should I look for when picking the perfect spot for my garden?

A: In short, when studying your yard to choose a garden plot, look for a level plot of land with good access to water and the appropriate amount of sunlight for the flowers you want to grow. Additionally, if some areas are more protected from animals (who may want to munch on your garden!) or from wind, these are optimal. After all, you don't want to plant your garden next to a structure that might cause a natural wind tunnel!

Q: Should I plant annuals or perennials?

A: When choosing whether to plant annuals or perennials, keep in mind that perennial cut flowers are usually more of a long-term investment. This is because perennials, such as peonies and roses, often take a season or two to produce ample blooms. Most cut flowers are considered annuals (although many you could keep in the ground, which we'll discuss more in the individual flower profiles). Assume that most of your cut flowers will be annuals and will need replanting the next season. Replanting allows flowers to produce long, sturdy stems that are perfect for cutting and arranging.

Q: Should I plant in my front- or backyard?

A: Something to keep in mind when planning your garden is your local city requirements. Some cities and towns have rules and regulations on where you can build garden structures in your yard. Also keep in mind that if you are a member of a homeowners' association, there might be guidelines to where you can garden as well. Although they're rare, it's a good idea to check if any requirements apply to you before you begin building.

Q: How far apart should I space my plants?

A: When planning your garden spacing, always refer to your seed packet. The correct spacing should be listed for each plant variety. (In chapter 4, we will look specifically at how to read a seed packet.) Additionally, you can always reference the flower profiles in this book. Lastly, if you are a visual learner and a bit techy, there are many garden planning apps and websites that help you calculate the correct spacing. My personal favorite garden planner can be found on Almanac.com under "Gardening." There you can create a virtual blueprint of your gardening space and choose from a long list of flower and vegetable varieties to include. Once plants are added to your garden layout, the planner automatically shows how many plants you can fit with correct spacing in your garden.

Q: How do I know whether to start seeds indoors or outside?

A: The back of your seed packet will tell you about a flower's germination, harvesting, and planting, including whether or not to start it indoors and transplant or direct sow. If in doubt, you can check this book's flower profiles. Again, in chapter 4, we will look at how to read a seed packet, as well as how to start seeds indoors.

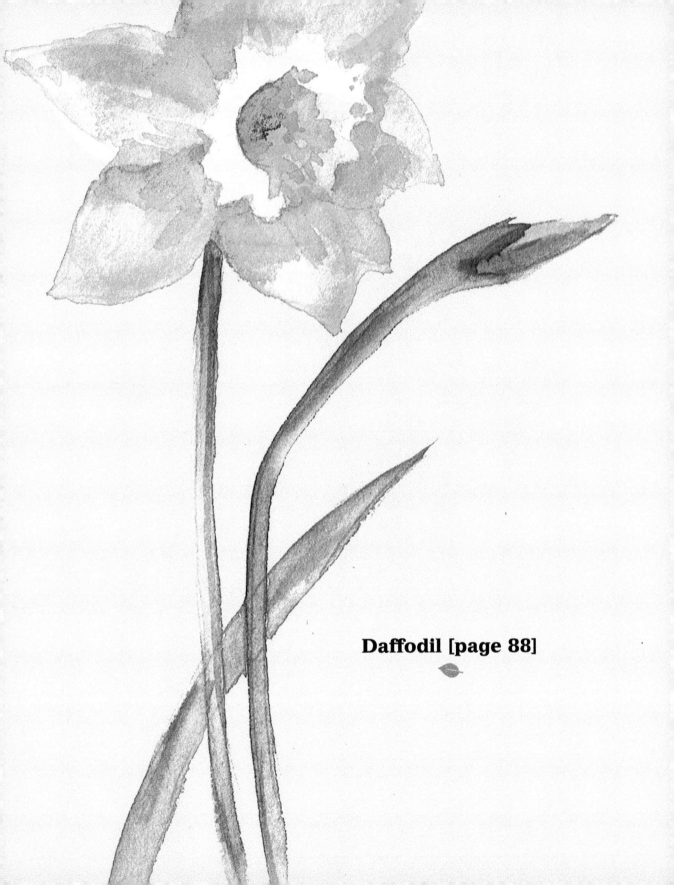

Daffodil [page 88]

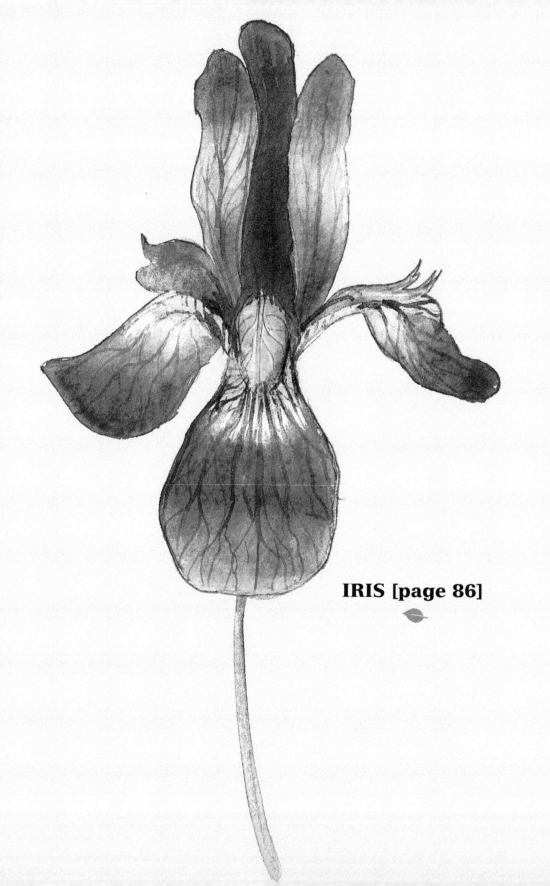

IRIS [page 86]

3

Setting up Your Flower Garden

Now that we've gone over the basics of planning your garden, it's time to start planting! Although the idea of building your garden beds might seem daunting, with some basic information, you'll be ready to confidently start your flower growing journey. You may even find that you have many of the necessary materials already. In this chapter, we will go into depth on how to set up the perfect growing environment for your plants. Starting from the ground up, we'll examine what type of soil will best feed your plants, followed by what type of garden will best suit your flower growing needs.

The Dirt on Dirt

You know the saying "you are what you eat"? Well, it definitely applies to flowering plants. Choosing the ideal type of soil will help your plants get the proper nutrients and bloom into a beautiful garden. If you are unfamiliar with gardening, it may seem like all dirt is the same. However, there is much to be learned about the delicate balance of the soil world. It is rare that the soil already in your ground is ready for growing, so learning how to blend your own is key for helping plants flourish. Fortunately, with just a few basic steps, you can easily create your own nutritious soil blend.

Soil Types Flowers Love

The success of your flower harvest starts with the soil. Although some plants vary in their soil needs, most flowering plants have similar requirements. There are three key elements to consider when choosing your garden soil. First, look for a soil that is well-draining, like sandy loam. Sandy loam soil is named after one of its key ingredients: sand. Sand is a common element in soil and allows for excess water to drain easily so that your plants don't drown. Second, look for a soil that has some water retention. Although this seems to contradict the first point, you do want your soil to retain *some* water to prevent your plants from becoming dehydrated. Lastly, choose soil that is nutrient-dense. These nutrients generally come from compost and fertilizer, which can be added to your soil blend. Aim to use natural compost, which can be found at your local feed or garden store. Oftentimes you'll find manure as a common compost ingredient. Manure makes a great natural compost for your soil by adding nutrients such as nitrogen, phosphorus, and potassium to it. When looking for compost, you're sure to find a "raised bed mix" or "garden mix" at your local garden shops. As long as you follow these guidelines, you're off to a great start.

Establish Soil Type and Check Soil Quality

Before you start growing, whether it be your first or tenth season, it is always a good idea to test your soil. Knowing your soil's nutrient balance can help you decide if you need to add any amendments to ensure your soil is optimal for growing. To check for soil quality, you can either do an at-home test or send away a soil sample to a lab. Either option is inexpensive and easy to do. For at-home testing, I like to use the Luster Leaf Rapitest kit. Once your soil has been tested, you'll want to look for three measurements: pH balance, nitrogen, and phosphorus. The pH of your soil will reveal whether your soil is more acidic or alkaline. A common at-home test usually gives you a guide of 3 to 10 on the pH scale. Generally, a pH of 6 or 7 for your soil is ideal for cut flowers; however, many seed packets will give you a better idea of what is best for a specific plant. Nitrogen is key for your plants' photosynthesis process, so you want to ensure that you have around 40ppm (parts per million or milligrams per liter) in your soil. Similarly, phosphorus helps your plants root and flower, so having a range of 25 to 50ppm of this nutrient in your soil is essential.

What Type of Garden Should You Have?

With your plot picked out, now it's time to decide how you are going to grow your garden. Containers, raised beds, or directly in the ground are all common types of garden foundations. In this section, we'll look at each option and decide which one fits your growing needs best. All these methods of gardening are easy to achieve and can be built for all your garden beds or mixed and matched. Determining your growing space may also lead you toward one garden design over another. However, all these garden foundations are wonderful ways to start establishing a flourishing cut flower garden.

In-Ground Gardening

If you aren't wanting to commit to building a raised bed or a container garden just yet, try your hand at growing straight in the ground. An in-ground garden is one in which the garden rows are built directly on top of your existing ground. This is a popular choice for beginning gardeners and established growers alike because it is cost-effective, space-saving, and quick to establish, as you don't need lumber to build a bed, just soil, compost, and recycled cardboard. However, there are a few things to know when opting for an in-ground garden. First, because the garden bed is directly on the ground, it can lead to more interference from pests, such as rodents and bugs. Additionally, sometimes in-ground gardens have a harder time draining than raised-bed or container gardens, as they have less space to drain into. Even so, in-ground gardening is an accessible, easy place to start.

How to Make Your Own Soil Mix

If you're interested in a more controlled, hands-on approach to soil, try mixing your own! Creating your own soil recipe is beneficial, as it ensures that your soil fits your unique gardening needs. When creating your own garden soil mix, you want to create a blend that allows for the proper amount of drainage, moisture, and organic nutrients.

Coconut coir or leaf mold: Your basic garden soil needs to be well-draining so that your plants don't suffocate or rot. To ensure proper drainage, add one part coconut coir or leaf mold to your soil mix. Coconut coir is the outer fiber found on coconut shells, whereas leaf mold is the remnants of decomposing leaves. Both add aeration to your soil and are also great alternatives to using peat moss, which is a natural resource that needs to be preserved in our ecosystems.

Topsoil: Found naturally or bought bagged, topsoil is essential in your soil mix. It makes up the top 6 to 8 inches of soil found naturally in the ground and is especially rich in nutrients because of the decaying matter it comes into contact with, such as leaves and other organic materials. It has a great moisture content and retention that will help keep your plants hydrated. Add one part topsoil to your soil mix.

Compost: To provide your soil mix with organic nutrients, finish it off with one part compost. This could be compost you made yourself, store-bought, or even manure from a local farm. Compost will add the rich nutrients needed to feed your plants.

After mixing these three ingredients together in a 1:1:1 ratio, you will have a great standard garden soil mix! For a simple consistency check, pack your soil into a ball. It should keep its shape when held and crumble when poked. If it doesn't, add more water if it is too dry or more topsoil if it is too damp.

Container or Raised Bed?

After in-ground gardening, the two most common designs for beginner gardeners are container and raised-bed gardens.

Raised beds are typically wood structures that frame in soil to create a thick, healthy layer of dirt above the open ground. They are great for proper drainage and, when filled with quality soil, help your plants thrive. However, it is worth noting that raised beds can be expensive and time-consuming, since they have to be constructed. There are up-front costs to factor in for the materials and soil, and there can also be some minor maintenance year to year involved in the upkeep of your beds and topping off your soil.

Container gardening is perfect for those with small spaces or in need of a portable garden option. These gardens are easily planned and super accessible, no matter the space. Furthermore, a wide variety of plants can thrive in containers such as pots, buckets, or galvanized tubs. However, these containers are fully enclosed, so lack of drainage and root development can be a disadvantage of container gardening.

Figuring Out Size and Shape

When determining the size of your garden, remember that a bountiful cut flower yield can come from a small space. For raised beds, try starting out with two beds measuring 3 feet wide, 6 feet long, and 1 foot deep. Leave enough space between the beds for you to easily pass through and harvest. For containers, try growing in galvanized tubs. Seventeen-gallon tubs that measure 2 feet wide and 5 feet long are perfect and can be found at any hardware or farm store. Four buckets and one or two galvanized tubs will be plenty of space to get you started with a nice, small cutting garden.

Mixing and Matching Garden Types

Still not sure which type of garden to grow? Good news: You don't have to only choose one! Mixing and matching garden types is a great way to maximize space and grow to specific plant needs. Some plants, like dahlias, prefer to have the depth and drainage of a raised bed, whereas many herbs and bulbs are happy to live in a container. For plants such as tulips, containers can protect them from pests. Containers can also prevent plants like mint and nasturtiums from spreading and reseeding to your whole garden. Experiment with your space, and don't be afraid to try a combination to see what feels right for you.

How to Create an In-Ground Garden

Once you've decided to start an in-ground garden, it's time to prepare, plant, and fill your space. To do so, you will need a few key materials and concise instructions, outlined here. Please note that for in-ground gardens, I recommend using a "no-till" method. Tilling is when you dig up or turn over your lawn or soil, and it is sometimes recommended with in-ground gardening. However, as I outline in the FAQ section (see page 36), it can cause problems in the long term, so follow the process here instead.

Materials and Tools Needed

Be sure to have the following materials on hand before you start.

Rake: A rake can be used to loosen the soil before planting or to mix in compost into the top layer of soil.

Hoe: A hoe is useful for making a small trench when planting a large quantity of bigger seeds.

Pen: Pens are perfectly sized for creating a small hole for your seeds. They can also be used with your labels.

Mister: A hose with a mist setting or a handheld mister is necessary to gently water your seedlings after planting.

Labels: When planting seeds, it's helpful to remind yourself what you planted where. Use stakes or labels to organize your growing space.

Preparing Your Site

1. A few weeks before you'd like to plant, lay a tarp or some cardboard down over the piece of land where you want to garden. Keep it there for a few weeks, during which it will naturally kill the grass or weeds you may have growing in your plot.

2. Once the space is clear, remove the tarp or cardboard and lay down a piece of recycled cardboard the size of your ideal plot.

3. Pile a good 7-inch mound of soil and compost all over the top of the cardboard. (The cardboard will act as a barrier to weeds and will naturally decompose with time.)

4. Rake the soil lightly to mix it without disrupting it too much.

5. Thoroughly mist the soil all over. It should be damp to the touch to ensure there is moisture ready to hydrate the seeds. Sometimes I even like to water my soil a few days before I plant to ensure deeper hydration for the seeds.

Planting and Filling

After your in-ground garden is prepared, I suggest performing a quick soil check before you plant. Is your soil damp but not soaked? Is the soil loose enough to promote good drainage? If you answered yes to both questions, then you're ready to move on to planting. The biggest consideration when planting an in-ground garden is which flowers will naturally perform better under these conditions. Some of these flowers include hydrangeas, lilacs, and spirea. They are successful for in-ground gardening because these cut flowers are shrubs and need to develop over a few years. In-ground gardening offers a more permanent home for these flowers where you can develop them as abundant cut flowers for years to come.

How to Create a Container Garden

If growing a container garden is right for you, you will first need to purchase a few materials and then modify your containers for drainage. Follow the steps here to get started. A quick note on finding containers: if you search "container gardening online," you'll likely find ones that cost anywhere from $200 to $300 per container. Don't be discouraged! There are many inexpensive options available that still look put together. One of my favorite go-to containers for growing flowers is a 17-gallon galvanized tub. At about $25 each, they are an inexpensive way to add a couple of tubs of flowers to a deck or patio. Really, anything that will hold your soil, can have holes drilled into it, and fits in your location can work. Get creative and work with what you have.

Materials and Tools Needed

Make sure to have these tools for your container garden.

Soil: As with raised beds, a well-draining soil is key to ensure the moisture doesn't stay trapped in your container.

Compost: Mix compost into your soil and add another layer on top.

Container: Many containers will work, but look for one that you can plant multiple flowers in. A 17-gallon tub, a 44-gallon stock tank, or even plastic 31-gallon storage containers that you might already have at home will all work.

Electric drill: You will use this to drill drainage holes in the base of your containers.

Plastic mesh or weed cloth: By lining the base of your container, you allow water to escape, but not soil.

Wood blocks: Although not necessary, blocks can be placed under the container to lift it off your deck and provide more airflow and drainage.

Preparing and Modifying Containers

1. Collect your containers and know their width, length, and height measurements. This will help you determine how many drainage holes you will need.

2. Prepare to drill drainage holes in the bottom of your containers. You will need an electric drill, appropriate drill bit pieces, protective eyewear, and a marker to mark your holes.

3. Mark your drainage holes, starting with one in the center of the base, and then one every 4 to 6 inches in either direction. The bigger the container, the more drainage holes are needed.

4. Drill your marked holes ¼ to ½ inch in diameter. Make sure you are wearing a mask so that you do not inhale any materials, as well as protective eyewear.

5. After drilling, line the base of your containers with mesh, burlap, or weed cloth. The material should allow water to drain through but prevent soil from escaping. Fit it to the base and cut off any excess.

6. Place your containers where you would like them prior to filling them with soil. (Once filled, they'll be heavy!)

7. Fill your lined containers with well-draining soil. Mix in compost, then top with extra compost to feed your seedlings. Your containers are ready for planting!

Filling Your Containers

As mentioned in previous sections, when planting in a raised bed or container, pick a soil that drains excess moisture, retains enough moisture, and feeds your plants with nutrients. Additionally, it is important to monitor your containers' garden soil throughout the season. Containers are prone to water retention, which can rot the roots of your plants. If it seems that your container is holding on to too much water, adjust your watering or create more drainage holes. Plants that grow particularly well in containers include tulips, marigolds, and zinnias.

How to Create a Raised-Bed Garden

Raised beds are a foolproof way to start your own cut flower garden. By building a raised structure on top of your garden site, you can control not only their depth, but also how level they are and what soil you use. Raised beds are often the most expensive option to start a cut flower garden; however, with the right materials, your raised beds will last for years to come and provide a safe space for your flowers to grow. Most raised beds are constructed out of wood, and even if you do not have building experience, you will be able to make your own raised bed. The tools needed to build are common and you most likely have them already. However, borrowing tools or renting them are also good options. In this section, you will find step-by-step instructions and illustrations on how to build your own raised beds.

Preparing Your Site

When choosing your site, ensure that it is level so that it is easy to install your beds. If your site is not level, leveling it is your first step for proper preparation. To do so, add or subtract soil until the angle of your bed is less severe. If your site is level, measure it. Most beds are 3 feet wide and 6 feet long. Using a string and stakes, you can mark out the area that you plan on building. Once your area is marked, prepare the soil by smothering any grass or weeds with a tarp or cardboard. Leave those on for a few weeks until the grass has died back, then you're ready to build.

Materials and Tools Needed

These basic materials will help you build your own raised beds.

Electric drill: A drill will save you time and effort while screwing together the raised beds.

Screws: These are for holding the wood of your beds together.

Tape measure: A tape measure is essential for making correct measurement marks on your wood and to plan out your space.

Hand saw: Although you can use an electric saw, a hand saw will do the trick.

Wood: There are multiple varieties of wood that can be used to build your beds. Pine, cedar, and hemlock are all commonly used, with cedar being the top choice in terms of longevity. Avoid treated woods, because the chemicals will leach into your soil.

Cardboard or weed cloth: Place at the bottom of your bed to prevent grass or weeds from growing into your bed.

Building Your Raised Bed

1. Gather your supplies. For an average-size rectangular raised bed, you will need six 6-foot-long planks of 2-by-6-inch wood. You will also need a 6-foot-long 2-by-2-inch piece of wood. Your finished bed will be 1 foot deep, 3 feet wide, and 6 feet long, and the walls will be 2 inches thick. Although these plans are for that size, you can easily adjust them to create any size to fit your space.

2. Cut two of the 2-by-6-inch boards in half to create four 3-foot-long 2-by-6-inch boards. These will be the short sides of the planter. Cut the 6-foot-long 2-by-2-inch piece of wood into four 1 ½-foot-long sections. These will act as the corner braces.

3. Lay down two of the 6-foot-long 2-by-6-inch boards horizontally on the ground, so that their long sides are touching. Lift up the ends of the planks and slide two of the 1½-foot-long corner pieces beneath them. The corner stakes should rest at the left and right edges of the planks and be level with the top of the upper plank with a half foot of the stake poking down beneath the bottom plank. Screw the long-side boards to the corner stakes using two screws per plank end (for a total of eight screws).

4. Repeat step 3 with the remaining two 6-foot-long 2-by-6-inch boards and two 1½-foot-long corner pieces. You now have both long sides of the planter built.

5. Once you have the two long sides of the planter prepared, flip them over (with the stakes pointing up at the sky) to attach the shorter sides. The sides of the planter walls with the corner stakes should be facing each other, and the planter walls should stand about four feet apart. (It helps to have an extra set of hands here.)

6. Place one 3-foot-long 2-by-6-inch piece of wood standing upright against the edges of the two long sides with their corner braces. Screw the wood into the corner brace with two screws per edge (for a total of four screws). Stack another 3-foot-long 2-by-6-inch piece of wood on top of the last one so that it also touches the sides of the long walls and corner braces. Screw it onto the corner braces with two screws per side (for a total of four screws). One of the short planter walls is now attached.

7. Repeat step 6 with the remaining two 3-foot-long 2-by-6-inch boards so that your planter has four connected walls, complete with 6-inch-long corner brace "stakes."

8. Flip your bed so that the stakes are now touching the ground. Place the bed in your ideal location, then dig a small hole beneath each corner stake. Place the corner stakes into the holes and then fill in any remaining space in the holes with dirt to secure and stabilize the bed. The bottom of the flower bed sides should be touching the ground.

9. Line the bottom of your bed with cardboard or weed cloth, then fill to the top with soil and compost (these will settle to a lower level with time and weather). Congratulations! You're now ready to plant.

Filling and Sectioning Your Raised Bed

Fill your raised bed with quality, well-draining soil and your flower beds will thrive. You can find bags of raised bed soil mixes at the store; however, if you are filling more than one bed, check out a local landscaping company for a soil delivery. This option is often cost-effective, and the soil is high quality. Mix in high-quality compost to ensure that your plants get the nutrients they need, and you're ready to select what flowers to plant.

Compost and Mulch

Compost and mulch are the magic ingredients to keeping your plants well-fed and thriving. To note the difference, compost is mixed into the soil to add nutrients, whereas mulch is added as a protective layer on top of the soil. Often compost is added to garden beds prior to planting and then refreshed yearly to add nutrients back into your garden. Mulching is done at various stages, but typically in the early spring and fall.

When choosing a compost for your garden, organic is always best. You can purchase organic compost at your local garden center; one of my favorite all-purpose composts is G&B Organics Soil Building Conditioner. You may also be able to find free compost near you on neighborhood sharing websites.

Additionally, creating your own compost is a great way to repurpose food and organic scraps into something of value. To create a compost pile, clear a space and spread out a layer of straw to promote aeration. Start with a base of some preestablished compost and then add scraps like fruits, veggies, eggshells, coffee, and leaves. Turn your pile every few weeks and add nitrogen to expedite the composting process. (Grass clippings or coffee grounds are both easy, accessible sources of nitrogen for compost piles.) Find more information about starting your own compost pile in the Resources section (page 160).

To mulch, top your soil with organic materials such as leaves, shredded bark, or grass clippings, which will insulate your soil against weeds and retain its moisture.

When planting in your raised beds, select flowers that have similar growing conditions, watering needs, and heights so that they will complement one another in a shared growing space. In some cases, you may want to plant your garden bed with all one flower type in different varieties. For example, zinnias come in lots of shapes and colors; why not plant a bed with a few variations? If you are wanting to plant different flower varieties in one bed, keep in mind that spacing and height variation matters. If planted together, tall plants such as cosmos and dahlias could block out the light of smaller plants like calendulas and nigellas. Plant with sunlight, spacing, and size in mind, and you will have diverse, colorful flower beds to harvest from!

FAQ: Building a Flower Garden

Check out some of the most common questions about building your flower garden.

Q: What containers are best for flowers?

A: As long as your containers and flower beds are deep enough to allow space for ample root growth and drainage, flowers are adaptable and can grow in many different container environments. The more space the better, but experiment and see what works best for you. For my garden, I grow in both raised beds and containers with no problems. I often reserve container growing for spring bulbs such as tulips, ranunculus, and anemones; however, I have had success with dahlias and sweet peas in containers as well. Raised beds and in-ground growing are great for every flower variety, so you can't go wrong with those.

Q: How deep should I build my flower beds?

A: Twelve inches is standard. Dahlias, for example, need to be planted 6 inches deep with room for tubers and roots to grow. Any less and the root system would be crowded and underdeveloped. When building your raised beds, many wood pieces come precut at 6 inches wide, making it simple to create a 1-foot-deep bed. It can be more difficult to find containers at that depth; however, most galvanized troughs and buckets will work well.

Q: How often should I refresh my raised bed soil?

A: The base of your soil can stay the same for many years; however, after each growing season, the nutrients in your soil are depleted. To solve this problem, top your flower beds with organic mulch, such as leaves or grass clippings, to help prevent soil erosion. You can also consider planting a cover crop. A cover crop is a plant that is seeded into your soil with the intention of only covering the soil to add nutrients back to it and then pulled out before spring planting. Common cover crops are hairy vetch and red clover. If you choose to leave your soil as is during the winter, amend it in the spring with quality compost. Refreshing your soil with a few inches of compost on top will add the essential nutrients back into it, and you'll be ready to plant for the next season.

Q: What do the numbers on fertilizer bags mean?

A: The three numbers on a fertilizer bag represent the three main nutrients found in the mix. The first number is the percentage of nitrogen, the second number is the percentage of phosphorus, and the third number is the percentage of potassium. The best way to figure out what fertilizer number is best for your garden is to do a soil test. Soil testing is the only sure way to know which key nutrients might be low and need to be added. When choosing a blend, select an organic fertilizer; chemical fertilizers are often toxic to pets and children, not to mention all the natural pollinators in your garden. *Down to Earth* brand fertilizers are organic and can be found at your local garden shop. This brand's 4-1-3 all-purpose fertilizer is a great place to start.

Q: Don't I need to dig up the ground before placing a flower bed?

A: Digging up the ground you intend to garden, or "tilling" it, can provide temporary fertility for your soil, but it is not long-lasting. Tilling the ground not only disrupts the natural ecosystem in your soil but can also increase your weeds and deplete your soil's nutrition and volume over time. Instead, leave the soil where you intend to plant undisturbed, even if you decide to plant in the ground. Follow the directions on page 49 for an environmentally conscious start to your cut flower garden.

ROSE [page 126]

POPPY [page 96]

4

Plant Like a Pro

In my first year of gardening, I started all my seeds the same way. At the time, I was shocked when hardly any of them germinated and the ones that *did* germinate died. Oops! If I had made a plan, I could have had a flower garden that year. So that you don't make the mistakes I did, this chapter outlines how to plant your seeds for success. Although you'll also find specific planting details in the flower profiles, the following sections will provide general information about how to start from seed, direct sow, and plan out your garden beds.

Plant with a Plan

Now that you have an idea of what and where you want to plant, it is time to start planning out your cut flower garden. Plan out your flower garden in your journal so that it can be easily referenced during the growing season. When planning, also make sure to use the flower profiles in this book and your seed packets to gather the right information for each flower variety. Follow these steps to make a plan:

1. List the flowers that you want to grow. From this list, divide it into two categories: "must-grow" and "would like to grow." Remember to start with a few varieties that you love—and that you don't have to overcommit on your first season.

2. From there, divide these flowers into growing seasons. Most flowers will fit into spring or summer, but others may be in the fall.

3. For each plant, decide if you want to start your own seeds or purchase plant starters.

4. Write down the important dates for starting each flower variety. This should include the date to start your seeds indoors, the transplant date, and any direct sow dates.

5. Look up the recommended plant spacing for your flowers to decide how many to plant per flower variety. This can be found on the back of your seed packets.

6. For raised or in-ground beds, sketch a layout grid of your garden space. If using containers, draw a top view of each container. Your sketches should be drawn using some form of scale; for example, 1 inch = 1 foot.

7. Using a pencil and the correct spacing, mark where you will plant each flower. Put flowers with similar sun and water requirements together.

8. Label your sketches. Make sure to include the names of each variety you are planting and whether you will be direct sowing or not.

9. If you'd like, use colored pencils to sketch what your garden will look like in bloom.

6 ft

3 ft

Dahlias   Zinnias

Figure Out Your Last Frost Date

Most flower gardens begin and end with their frost dates. Your first and last frost dates are the average expected dates in the fall and spring, respectively, when the temperature is below 32°F. Most cut flowers do not fare well in freezing weather, so the flower season concludes with what we call the "killing frost," a hard freeze that kills your plants for the winter. In this chapter, you will need to know your region's last frost date in order to prepare for planting. Generally, seedlings and seeds can be planted outside around the last frost date. To find your region's last frost date, consult a planting almanac online or from your local library or call your local farm bureau. I find the quickest and easiest way to locate frost dates is to visit Almanac .com and search for your zip-code-specific dates.

Quantity and Spacing

When planning out your garden beds, it is important to space your plants correctly and identify the quantity of plants needed to fill your bed. "Quantity" of plants refers to how many seedlings you can plant in your bed with accurate spacing, whereas "spacing" refers to how far apart you need to plant them. It is important not to over-crowd your flower beds by planting too close together, because your plants could become stunted with the lack of sunlight and not reach their full maturity. In contrast, if you space your plants too far apart, you are missing out on valuable garden space and flowers! Spacing requirements for each flower variety can be found on the back of your seed packet or in the flower profiles of this book. They will often read something like "sow seeds 8 inches apart." This means that each seedling will need to be planted 8 inches apart in either direction. To make things simple, plant in a grid formation. This will also help you calculate the quantity of a particular flower variety that you can grow in each bed. Following spacing guidelines will yield a lush, flower-filled garden.

Planting with Mature Flowers and Seedlings

If starting plants from seeds is intimidating, consider purchasing seedlings, or "plugs." Although seeds are the less expensive option, buying plant starters can save you time and effort. To ensure quality, seedlings are best purchased directly from a local farm. Nurseries sometimes carry seedlings and often carry mature versions of flowering plants. However, be wary, as many flower varieties at nurseries are intended for landscape gardening, rather than cut flower gardening. Always confirm before purchasing that the mature plant will grow long enough stems to be cut.

When looking for healthy seedlings, follow these tips:

Look for seedlings that are healthy and flourishing. Avoid seedlings that look leggy or wilted.

Note when the seedlings were planted. You want seedlings that are established, so make sure they are securely rooted in the soil.

Check the roots. You don't want your seedlings to be too "rootbound," meaning the roots have wrapped around themselves from being in the pot for too long.

Ask if the seedlings have been hardened off. You'll want to know if you need to get them acclimated to the outdoors before planting to avoid transplant shock.

Get a few more seedlings than you anticipate needing. It's not uncommon to lose some seedlings during a transplant, so it's helpful to keep extras on hand.

And when selecting a mature plant, follow these tips:

Avoid impulsive purchases. It can be tempting to buy a flowering plant that is blooming and healthy! However, confirm that it can grow in your space and you have room for it before taking it home.

Bigger is not always better. Check for young, healthy, new growth of leaves and buds.

Check the roots. As with seedlings, you don't want any rootbound plants.

Look out for rot or disease. Check the leaves for graying, spots, or yellowing along the veins.

Read the label. Confirm that the plant will grow in your garden and that the variety is intended for cut flowers.

Planting from Seeds

Starting plants from seed both is rewarding and can elongate your growing season when started indoors. To determine when to start from seed, always consult the back of your seed packet. However, most seed planting happens during the months of February, March, and April. In this section, we will discuss the two different ways to start your flowers from seeds: indoor seed starting and direct sowing. Although some flowers can be started either way, most plants need to be started one way or the other and which one is stated on the seed packet. With these step-by-step instructions, you can give your plants the healthy start they need to grow into prolific flowers.

Tools and Materials for Starting Seeds Indoors

Once you've read your seed packet and determined you need to start some seeds indoors, the next thing to do is gather the necessary materials. Here are a few basics to purchase or borrow. If they seem too pricey for your budget, check out Using Recycled Materials to Start Seeds (page 48).

Seed cells with drip tray and humidity cover: This should be your first purchase when starting seeds indoors. Find a 72- or 50-plug tray with a drip tray and dome. The drip tray should have no draining holes so that you can bottom water when the seedlings are small. "Bottom water" refers to pouring water in the base of the tray so that the soil can absorb from the bottom instead of getting watered from the top. At this stage, top watering may wash away the seeds.

Seed-starting mix soil: It is important to use designated seed-starting soil when starting seeds. Seed-starting mix can be found at any garden or feed store and has a light, aerated consistency, allowing plants to germinate easily.

Grow lights: Although specifically manufactured grow lights are not needed, your seedlings *will* need a consistent source of light. LED shop lights from your local hardware store provide the necessary beams and are much more cost-effective than grow lights. Ensure that your lights are long enough to reach the entire length of your trays; traditional trays will need two or three lights each.

Plant labels: It can be difficult to identify plants in their newly germinated stage, so labeling your plants is a must. When labeling, use a marker that won't rub off over time, and add the date on the back of the stake for a quick reference.

How to Read a Seed Packet

However you plan to plant your seeds, make sure that you have your seed packets handy to review the planting information. Though seed packets vary by supplier, most print the same basic information. Take note of the following key details:

Plant variety: What flower it is and what specific variety.

Description: How the flower will look when fully in bloom.

Germination rate: What percentage of seeds to expect will germinate.

Plant type: If the flower is an annual or perennial.

Height: How tall the flower will be at maturity.

Sun: What the plants' sun needs are. Usually, full sun or partial shade.

Days to maturity: How many days from planting you can expect to have your first bloom.

Spacing: How many inches needed in between each plant when planting.

Planting instructions: Information about if to start your seeds indoors or direct sow, along with if the seeds need light or not to germinate.

Harvesting: For flowers, some seed packets have harvesting information that may include the vase life of the cut flower.

Date: All packets will include the date or year in which they were packaged. If kept in the correct conditions, seeds can last a couple of years. However, newer seeds provide the best germination rate.

Starting Seeds Indoors

Follow these directions to get your new seeds started.

1. **Gather materials:** Set up your soil mixing station with a bucket or tray, soil, seed packets, seed trays, domes, and water.

2. **Prepare the soil:** In your bucket or tray, mix seed-starting soil with enough water to make it damp, but not sopping wet.

3. **Fill the seed trays:** Scoop out some soil and spread it over your seed tray cells, filling them all evenly. Tap the tray on the ground to help settle the soil.

Figure 1

4. **Plant your seeds:** For most flower seeds, poke a tiny divot with your finger into each cell of soil and drop in two seeds (see figure 1). Some bigger seeds, like nasturtium, will need a bigger hole, whereas tiny seeds such as snapdragons don't need a hole at all. Consult your seed packet or flower profiles to determine what is best.

5. **Label:** Label your trays or cells with the flower, the variety, and the date you planted.

6. **Top the seeds:** For most germination processes, gently sprinkle dry seed-starting soil or vermiculite on top of your seeds, lightly covering them. Again, consult your seed packet for any unique directions.

7. **Water:** Gently mist the top of your trays with water to moisten the soil and create humidity in your tray domes.

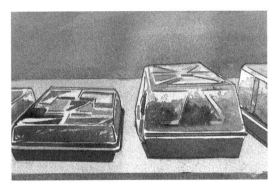
Figure 2

8. **Cover:** Cover your seed tray with a clear dome and place it somewhere that maintains a temperature between 68°F and 75°F (see figure 2).

9. **Monitor:** Check your seeds daily, and mist them with water as needed so they do not dry out. As soon as you see green from most of the plants sprouting, remove the dome.

10. **Light:** After removing the dome, place seed trays 3 to 5 inches below the grow lights (see figure 3).

Figure 3

11. **Check your seedlings:** Monitor your seedlings daily for moisture and development. Once the seedlings germinate, begin "bottom watering." Bottom watering is when you place the seed cells into a tray with water in it and the soil absorbs the water from the bottom. This protects the delicate seedlings from "above watering" that can sweep them away. After the soil has gathered moisture, carefully drain off the excess from the tray.

12. **Adjust:** As the seedlings grow, adjust your grow lights so that they are always 3 to 5 inches above the top of the seedlings. The lights should be close enough to prevent legginess, but not so close that they burn the seedlings.

Using Recycled Materials
to Start Seeds

Though you can buy the aforementioned seed-starting materials at your local garden store or online, you can also use things around your home to start seedlings. From recycled containers to free flowerpots, there are many different environmentally and budget-friendly options available.

Paper cups: One of the easiest ways to start seeds using recycled materials is in paper cups. Simply poke a few holes in the bottoms of the cups and fill with soil. Remove the seedlings from the cup before transplanting.

Yogurt containers: Individual yogurt containers are the perfect size for starting seeds. Carefully wash the containers and poke holes in the bottoms before planting.

Plastic flower pots: If you have been saving the plastic containers your plants come in, this is a perfect way to repurpose them. Most nurseries also have a pile of used ones that are free—just ask!

Newspaper pots: For a pot that you can plant directly into the ground, wrap a piece of newspaper around a soup can and fold it in place. Remove the can, leaving a cylinder of compostable newspaper.

Paper towel rolls: These rolls are a great option for seedlings that need room for their roots to grow, like sweet peas. They can also be planted directly into the soil.

In-Ground Gardening

There are many different reasons one might choose to direct sow instead of starting indoors. Some plants resent being transplanted, like larkspurs and sunflowers. Additionally, flowers like poppies, phlox, and cress are fragile and do best being planted directly into the soil. Some flowers, like zinnias, cosmos, and nasturtiums, are adaptable and can be started either way. Other flowers, like tulips and dahlias, are started from a bulb or tuber, which need to be placed directly into the soil. Keep a few key points in mind when planting and your direct sown plants will thrive.

1. **Prepare your seeds:** Some seeds may require an additional step before planting to wake them up. For example, sweet peas and nasturtium sometimes require a soak in water to soften the outer shell of the seeds. Look at the back of your seed packet for this information.

2. **Prepare the soil:** Following the guidelines in chapter 3 (see page 28), make sure you are starting with moist and conditioned soil.

Figure 4

3. **Review planting information:** Before planting your seeds, read up on the plant's light needs on the back of your seed packet. If seeds need less light to germinate, they will be planted in small holes; if they need more, they will be sprinkled on top of the soil (see figure 4).

4. **Plant your seeds:** If less light is needed, use a pen or your finger to poke properly spaced holes into the soil, about twice as deep as the seed size. Plant two seeds per hole to ensure the best germination rates. If more light is needed, sprinkle your seeds onto the soil according to the seed packet.

5. **Cover the seeds:** Most seeds can be covered with a gentle sprinkling of soil. Do not tamp it down. Some, as aforementioned, do not need to be covered at all. (An example of this is poppies.)

Figure 5

6. **Water:** Once your seeds are planted, use the mist setting on your hose to water them. Mist is perfect as it will not wash away your seeds. Keep the soil damp throughout the germination and growing process (see figure 5).

Transplanting Seedlings

If you have started your seedlings indoors, eventually you will need to transplant them outside into your garden beds. As the seedlings are tender and susceptible to shock at such a young age, it is important to follow these steps to ensure a successful transplant.

1. **Time it:** Using your last frost date, your plants' days to maturity, and your local weather as a guide, mark your calendar with the date when you expect to transplant your seedlings. Some plants, like sweet peas, are light-frost tolerant and can be planted outside before your last frost date. However, most plants cannot handle a freeze and will need to be planted out just after your scheduled last frost date. Use your last frost date as a guide, but be familiar with your local weather conditions at the time of planting. Heavy rains or winds can damage young seedlings, so use your best judgment when transplanting outside.

Figure 6

2. **Harden off:** All seedlings will need to be "hardened off," or acclimated to the outdoor temperatures. Until now, your seedlings have been cozied up indoors under the grow lights—without the proper transition into the outdoors, they can become stunted. Around 1 to 2 weeks before planting outside, start gradually bringing your seedlings outdoors. Make sure that your seedlings have three or four sets of true leaves to ensure they are old enough (see figure 6). Start with letting them rest outside for an hour at a time in partial sun, and

gradually build up to a full day and night. Rushing this process can kill your seedlings, so this step is essential.

Figure 7

3. **Plan your rows:** Following the planting guide in your journal, gently place the seedlings on top of the soil in your beds. This will help you visualize where the seedlings need to be planted and make it easier to adjust their placement (see figure 7).

4. **Prepare the soil:** Once you have determined where your seedlings will be planted, dig the holes. You can use a trowel to dig individual holes, or, if you are planting many seedlings at once, you can use a hoe and dig a trench. Once dug, give your soil a gentle spray with water to moisten the planting area.

Figure 8

5. **Plant the seedlings:** Place your seedlings in their respective holes, making sure not to disrupt their roots. Once set, pile the soil back around the base of the plant and gently tap down to secure (see figure 8).

6. **Water:** To help your seedlings acclimate and stay hydrated, gently water around the base of the plant once planted.

FAQ: Seed Starting and Planting

Lastly, let's dive into some commonly asked questions about starting seeds.

Q: **When should I start my seeds indoors?**

A: Generally, plan to start your seeds indoors 6 weeks before your final frost date. Some seeds may take longer to germinate, and some may take less time—consult your seed packet for a more detailed time frame. It is possible to start your seeds too soon, because they'll be ready to be transplanted before the outdoor conditions are safe. In this case, you may have to transplant your seedlings to a larger pot and keep them under the grow lights before you can transplant them outdoors.

Q: **When is the right time to direct sow seeds?**

A: To arrive at your direct sow date, consider your last frost date, the plant's days to maturity, and your local weather conditions. Generally speaking, the week after your region's last frost date is a good time to plan on direct sowing. Keep in mind your local weather at the time of planting—a week that is forecast to rain is not ideal for seeds, as they could become waterlogged or wash away. If you are in a region that encounters a lot of spring rain, such as the Pacific Northwest, consider investing in a caterpillar tunnel for your beds. A caterpillar tunnel is a small hoop tunnel that can be placed over seeds. Look for a tunnel that is covered with frost cloth rather than plastic so that it allows sunlight and water to still reach your seeds.

Q: **How long does it take for seeds to germinate?**

A: Germination times vary among different plant varieties. Environment conditions such as temperature, moisture, soil, and light can all affect germination times. Generally, a seed takes 7 to 10 days to germinate. Some plants, like sweet peas, are known to germinate quickly, whereas others, such as strawflowers, can take longer. Don't give up if you haven't seen shoots after 10 days—keep your soil moist and gently warmed, and you'll likely have germination success.

Q: How will I know when my seedlings are doing well?

A: Look for leaf development, color, and size on your seedlings to determine health. Seedlings should be compact and not overly leggy. If you see your seedlings elongating, try moving your grow light closer. If you see the leaves turning brown and crispy, they are getting burnt because the grow light is too close. Drooping can be a sign of underwatering, and yellowing can be a sign of overwatering. Check your seedlings every day to see how you may need to adjust their care.

Q: What is pinching?

A: Pinching is when you pinch out the center topmost sets of leaves when a seedling has three or four sets to encourage lateral growth. This can be done before you transplant your seedlings outdoors, or in some cases after. Consult the individual flower profiles or your seed packet for more information.

Q: None of my seeds germinated—now what?

A: If none of your seeds have germinated, don't get discouraged! It's time to do some investigating. First, confirm that you have waited long enough for them to germinate. Then confirm their light, water, soil, and temperature were all consistent with the recommendations. If everything seems right and it's still not working, plant another tray. Sometimes it takes a few tries to get it right.

Q: All my seeds germinated—now what?

A: It's time to thin your seedlings! None of us like to do it, but if you have more seedlings sprouted than you have space, don't try to cram them in. Simply thin by pulling out and discarding the extras. That will give the others the space they need to thrive.

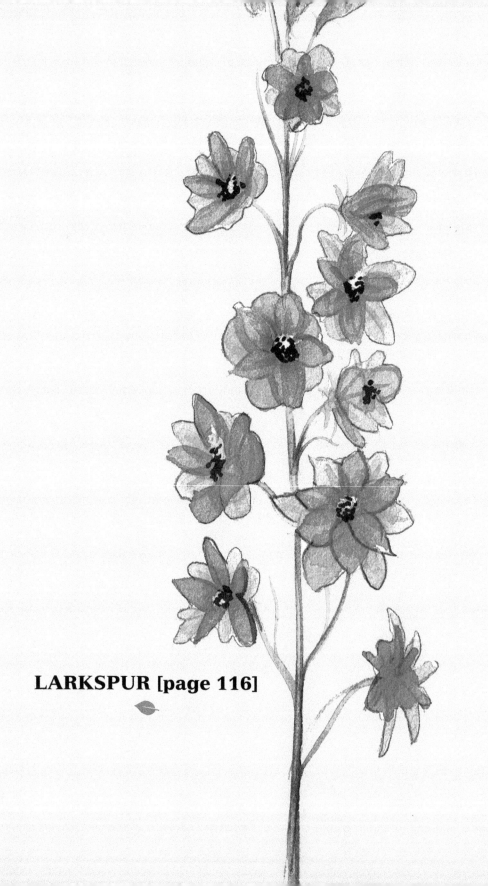

LARKSPUR [page 116]

5

Maintenance for Every Season

With some of the most challenging aspects of gardening behind you, it is now time to enjoy maintaining your flowers! Tending is the aspect of gardening that many fall in love with, as it is therapeutic to walk your garden rows, anticipating the new buds that are forming and caring for your growing plants. In this chapter, we will address how to care for your garden, get rid of any pests, and winter over your plots at the end of the season. There is always something to do in your garden, so read on to find out what your daily garden routine should look like after planting.

Basic Garden Care

There are many routine tasks involved in caring for your flower garden. After planting, the goal is not to only keep the plants alive but to also let them thrive. There are many simple tasks you can do to encourage a fantastic growing season. Since we are dealing with living plants, water, food, and upkeep are the simplest things you tend to in order to grow happy flowers. Make it a habit to allocate a small portion of your day to tending to your blooming garden. Your dedication will be rewarded with ample flowers to enjoy!

Watering

The essential element to any thriving garden is water. Keep your plants hydrated by watering directly at the roots and soil around the base of the plant. Overhead watering, or watering the plant as a whole, will not provide the hydration needed, and may damage flowers and leaves.

Depending on your garden, different watering systems might work best. Using a watering can is great for container gardens with smaller space, but a hassle for larger garden beds. Typically, a hose with different nozzle settings will save you time and energy, though you will have to remember to water your plants daily. If this is a concern for you, it may be worth investing in a simple irrigation system to water your plants on a timer. Drip irrigation can be easily set up from a kit and can automatically hydrate your plants thoroughly at the best hours.

For all systems, there is no need to water your garden when it has received a thorough rain. Overwatering your plants can also be a problem. To determine if your plants are getting the right amount of water, look for yellowing and limp leaves as signs of overwatering and browning of the leaves or stunted growth as signs of underwatering.

Pruning and Pinching

It often takes cutting back your plants to encourage new growth. Although most cut flower varieties don't require pruning, roses and peonies are two that benefit from this maintenance. Roses are often pruned in late winter or early spring, before the plant is blooming for the season. Cutting back leaves, dead branches, and crossing branches encourages healthy new growth from your rose, especially vertically. Read more about rose maintenance in the flower profiles.

Pinching is a technique widely used by gardeners to grow healthier, fuller plants that produce more blooms. Oftentimes a plant will send all its energy upward into the first singular stem it grows, resulting in a tall plant. To encourage the plant to produce more stems and grow outward, gardeners will cut back the plant in the early stages. Flowering plants, such as snapdragons, cosmos, zinnias, and dahlias, should all be pinched. Generally, wait for your plants that need pinching to have four or five leaf sets, then take a sharp set of garden scissors and cut across the center stem of the plant by cutting off the top of the plant, leaving two or three leaf sets. This will delay your first blooms, but the trade-off is more flowers in the long run. Reference the flower profiles to identify which flowers need to be pinched.

Weeding

Let me tell you up front that it is near impossible to have a weed-free garden. However, weeding should be on your weekly garden to-do list. When you weed on a regular basis, your plants won't be competing with imposters for space, nutrients, or sunlight.

The first way to help discourage weeds is to fill your garden bed with appropriately spaced plants. When your plants are spaced correctly, there should be little space between each plant once full-grown, preventing weeds from getting the light they'd need.

When pesky weeds do pop up, it is always best to remove them by hand rather than use herbicides. To a beginner's eye, it can sometimes be challenging to identify what is a weed and what is a sprout. Before you pull, check out the visuals at "13 Common Garden Weeds" at Almanac.com. When eradicating weeds, keep in mind that chemical herbicides are toxic to humans, animals, and insects and will disrupt the local ecosystem that your garden is a part of. Instead, take out your handy gloves and hoe and stay on top of your weeds the old-fashioned way.

Lastly, pulling weeds as you see them is much easier than trying to extract established weeds. Try pulling weeds when the soil is wet for easier removal. When your soil is dry, drag a hoe or weeding tool over the top to scrape out any rooted weeds.

Fertilizing

Before you fertilize your garden beds, it is important to know your soil nutrient levels. Always test your soil (a simple at-home test works great) to see what nutrients it needs so that you can make an educated decision on what to fertilize with.

All-purpose, organic fertilizer with equal levels of potassium, nitrogen, and phosphorus can help boost plant growth, though you may need a more specific fertilizer if one nutrient is particularly lacking.

Deadheading

Deadheading your flowers is an essential step to keeping your plants looking and feeling their best. To deadhead, simply cut or pinch off the head of any flowers that are past their blooming prime and going to seed. Staying on top of deadheading not only keeps your plants looking cleaner but also has many garden and flower production benefits. Leaving on the heads of flowers past their prime will encourage the plant to seed, expending the plant's energy and dropping seeds back into the soil. By deadheading, you are helping the plant put its energy back into making new blooms instead of caring for the dead ones, resulting in more flowers during the season.

Growing Up: Stakes, Cages, Trellises, and More

If you are growing climbing flowers, such as sweet peas or occasionally nasturtiums, you will need to provide vertical support for your flowers to climb. A wooden trellis purchased from your local garden store or a tuteur made out of sticks and twine will work perfectly. Some fences, such as chain-link fences, naturally provide wonderful support; however, you can also string twine vertically on your wooden fence to create supports. Many flowers, such as roses and dahlias, benefit from staking throughout the growing season. A simple wooden or metal stake will act as a support if the plant becomes tall and lopsided. Gently tie the stake with twine to the stem of the plant, or corral the plant by providing a twine "fence" that the plant can lean up against to provide support.

How to Cover Your Garden

Particularly when planting seedlings in the spring, your flowers may benefit from a bit of extra protection. Caterpillar tunnels are an easy, inexpensive way to protect your young plants from the elements. Find a caterpillar tunnel that is made with low hoops and frost cloth. This will protect your plants from harsh wind and rains, as well as against any surprise cold snaps. You can also create your own individual plant covers by cutting off the bottom of a plastic milk jug and using the top to cover your young plant. If you are covering your plants, make sure they are still getting the required amount of sunlight and water.

Tools for Sustaining Your Garden

Maintaining a healthy garden does not require many fancy tools; the essentials listed in chapter 1 will work wonderfully. However, there are a few nice-to-have tools that make maintaining and harvesting your garden even easier. These are not necessary for your first growing season, but they are worth looking into if gardening is something you want to commit to long-term.

Drip irrigation system: As previously mentioned, a timer-set drip irrigation system can be one secret to a successful garden, as it provides consistent watering close to the root system and you never have to worry about forgetting to water your plants. DripWorks provides beginner garden bed kits that are cost-effective and easy to put together.

Caterpillar frost cloth tunnel: When direct sowing seeds or planting spring bulbs such as anemones or ranunculus, it can be important to protect young sprouts from the elements. Find inexpensive options on Amazon!

Weeding tools: A handheld weeder or action hoe makes weeding quick and easy without requiring you to crouch down. These can also help pull from the root instead of simply taking off the top of the weed.

Garden belt: Especially during the blooming season, wearing a garden belt with clippers, twine, and labels can be handy when walking through your garden.

Kneeling pad: To protect your knees, a kneeling pad provides some cushion when tending to your soil. Even a towel can work in a pinch!

Troubleshooting the Root of Common Problems

Let's explore the solutions to some of the most typical beginner concerns regarding growing.

When will my first flowers bloom? There are a lot of factors that play into when you will get your first blooms. The planting date, days to maturity, pinching, and weather conditions all contribute to how long a plant takes to bloom. Keep in mind that if the weather has been hotter or cooler than average, that can affect your plant's growth. Additionally, plants that you have pinched are usually delayed by 2 weeks.

Why aren't my plants growing any bigger? If it seems as though your plants' growth is stunted, there are a few scenarios to explore. Extreme weather conditions can cause temporary stunting of plants, as well as under- or overwatering. Stunted growth may also be caused by lack of nutrients in the soil or by pests such as aphids. Do a soil test and look for pests to determine the cause. Often, stunted growth is associated with the water levels in the soil, so try watering different amounts to see if that helps.

Why are my leaves turning brown and dry around the edges? If you notice your plants' leaves are turning brown around the edges, they may be suffering from sunburns or fertilizer burns. Fertilizer burn can happen if your plants have been overconditioned, meaning that they are given an excess of minerals that are not needed. However, if caught early, overconditioning can be easily reversed. Simply remove the affected leaves and run water gently through your garden soil to wash any excess fertilizer away from your plants.

Why are my plant leaves yellow? Yellowing of leaves is a common occurrence and can mean many things. Yellow leaves can be a sign of underwatering, overwatering, a lack of nitrogen in your soil, pests, or disease. First, check your watering. If the leaves are yellow, soft, and droopy, they are being overwatered. If the yellowing is happening along the veins of the leaves, it is likely due to disease. If you suspect disease, there are apps and websites that can help you identify what it may be and how it can be helped, such as the pest and disease guides on Almanac.com.

Why are my plant stems curved? If your stems are all curved or bent, it might mean that they need more support. If you notice this happening, try staking your plants to correct the curve. Flowers such as snapdragons and phlox do well when supported by a net at an early stage. They can then grow through the tied, taut netting that acts as a stabilizer for their stems. When growing through a netting placed 8 inches or so above the ground, the plants will be encouraged to grow vertically and produce straight stems.

Pests and What to Do about Them

"If your garden doesn't have bugs, it isn't a part of the ecosystem." When I once asked a gardening friend how to get rid of my own garden pests, this was her wise response. She's right: both beneficial and pesky bugs are part of the garden process, and you're sure to have them. Follow these organic tips to keep your plants healthy while still preserving the pollinators and ecosystem. Also refer to the flower profiles for individual flower tips.

Aphids: A common garden pest, aphids are green or black insects that clump along tender, new growth. If left untreated, aphids can eat your flowers and stunt the growth of plants. To combat them, purchase ladybugs from your local feed store and release them at night on the affected plants. They will eat the aphids and play an important role in keeping garden pest populations at bay. Additionally, fertilizing your garden with worm castings releases the enzyme chitinase, which is toxic to aphids. Once they eat it, they will die. Bye, bugs!

Slugs: A well-known garden pest, slugs like to feast on leaves, chewing holes into your flowering plants. When spotted, slugs can easily be physically removed from the plant. However, Sluggo Plus is an organic insect repellent pellet that can be added on top of your soil to keep slugs at bay. Simply sprinkle it around the base of your plants to deter them.

Leafhoppers: Leafhoppers are slender green bugs that jump between your plants mid- to late season. They unfortunately can spread disease or viruses in your garden. To deter them, keep a clean garden space by picking up any decomposing plant matter. If you spot leafhoppers, you can also give your plants a powerful water bath to drench the bugs and dislodge them from the leaves.

Powdery mildew: If you notice a gray or white powder covering the stems and leaves of your plants, it is likely a common fungal infection called powdery mildew. In the short term, remove the affected leaves and treat it with a store-bought or homemade organic fungicide (see page 127). To avoid it completely in the future, create airflow through your plants and don't let the foliage become excessively moist.

Deer and rabbits: Although cute, these animals love to eat the leafy greens of plants and flowers. The simplest way to keep out deer and rabbits is by fencing off your garden. Creating a protective barrier using chicken wire will often keep these animals from getting to your leafy greens. However, you can also use predator pee as a natural deterrent, because the animals will think there is a predator near your garden. Maine Outdoor Solutions supplies predator urine from animals such as coyotes, bears, and foxes. When you spray it on your garden, rabbits and deer will steer clear.

Earwigs: These pests love to chew holes through leaves and flowers, especially dahlias. To trap them, leave out an empty tuna can filled with water near the base of your plants. The earwigs will be attracted to the smell and become trapped in the water.

Year-Round Care

Although the peak of your garden will be the blooming season, there are many tasks that make that prolific season happen. Garden jobs carry over from season to season, and maintaining a flower garden is a year-round task. From seed selection to garden cleanup, you can expect to complete a few simple gardening chores each month of the year. Here you will find a general checklist of *tasks* to be completed each season. Though these are common, check with your regional farming almanac or local gardeners to see what tasks may be regionally specific for you.

Early Spring

You've done all your planning over the winter, and now it's time to make your garden happen. During the months of February and March, gardeners are preparing their garden beds outdoors and starting seeds indoors. How you prepare during these months will directly affect your summer flower harvests.

☐ **Prepare soil:** After your soil has been sitting all winter, it is time to amend it. To determine what amendments will benefit your beds, send away for a soil test or do one at home. When the results are ready, prepare your soil with compost, amendments, or mulch to get them ready for seedlings in the coming weeks.

☐ **Start seeds indoors:** For summer blooms, it is time to start your seeds indoors. Most flowers take 90 to 100 days from germination to first bloom, so February and March are the perfect time to start. Make sure you are only starting flowers that can be transplanted after the frost.

☐ **Plant frost-tolerant spring blooms:** Some flowers, such as sweet peas, can be direct sown before the last frost date. Now is the time to plant! If you did not get a chance in the fall to plant your spring bulbs, such as tulips and ranunculus, you can also plant in the early spring to get a shorter harvest.

☐ **Prepare garden beds:** If this is your first year growing a cut flower garden, early spring can be a great time to design and build your flower beds for summer flowers. Make sure that your beds are built before you have to transplant your seedlings. In later years, consider expanding your garden at this time as well.

☐ **Purchase summer bulbs and tubers:** If you are planning on growing lilies, dahlias, or gladiola during the summer months, now is the time to purchase the bulbs and tubers. Find them online or at your local garden center.

Late Spring

If you are growing spring flowers, late spring is an exciting time, as it marks the first harvest! Even if you did not grow spring flowers this season, late spring is a wonderful time when gardeners start working in their garden beds, preparing for summer blooms.

☐ **Direct sow seeds:** The late spring (after the last frost) is an ideal time to direct sow the flowers that do best when planted directly into the soil. Check the seed packet for planting requirements and date recommendations. If temperatures are still cool, consider a frost-cloth caterpillar tunnel to protect your seeds and seedlings.

☐ **Thin indoor seedlings:** Indoor seeds will have germinated by now, and it is time to focus on preparing healthy seedlings for planting. If multiple seeds germinated in the same hole during direct sowing or indoor planting, thin out the seedlings by pulling out all but one. This will provide that one with the room needed to grow.

☐ **Transplant seedlings:** After any fear of a frost has passed, follow the directions outlined in the flower profiles or on the back of your seed packet to transplant your seedlings outside. Make sure you have hardened off your seedlings so that they are ready for the outdoor conditions.

- ☐ **Spring harvest:** If you planted spring bulbs in the fall, now is the time to harvest! Flowers such as tulips and narcissus provide one flower per bulb. You can cut these at the base, leaving the bulb in for next year, or pull up the entire plant and compost the bulb.

- ☐ **Weed:** While your flower beds are empty and the seedlings are small, make sure to stay on top of weeding. Use either your hands or a small weeding tool to clear invasive plants so that your seedlings have the space to grow.

Early Summer

During the early months of summer, the flower harvest season begins to take off. Now is the time to tend to your growing plants to ensure they stay healthy and produce many flowers. In most zones, the weather begins to heat up during this time of year, so gardeners prepare their gardens for warmer temperatures.

- ☐ **Pinch select seedlings:** Once your seedlings have multiple sets of healthy leaves, it is time to pinch. Not all flowers will need pinching, so confirm which will benefit before snipping.

- ☐ **Plant fall flowers:** If you are planning to grow fall flowers, plant your seedlings now. Depending on your growing zone, flowers such as dahlias need to be planted around the beginning of June. You can also sow a second succession of summer flowers, such as zinnias, snapdragons, and celosia, that will last into the fall months.

- ☐ **Harvest flowers:** Summer means harvest season! Keep buckets and clippers at the ready so that you can do a bit of harvesting daily. When harvesting, make sure to place snipped stems directly in cool, fresh water to hydrate them and keep them alive longer.

- ☐ **Flip garden beds:** Some gardeners plant two seasons of flowers in one bed. If you grew spring flowers and are now wanting to grow fall flowers, dig up any bulbs and prepare your soil with compost and amendments.

- ☐ **Deep water:** Most growing zones during the summer months experience a raise in temperature. When expecting a heat wave, make sure to deeply water your plants by watering for a longer period to allow it to reach deep down to the roots. Warmer weather means you need to water more, so adjust your schedule accordingly.

Late Summer

Late summer is a magical time for gardeners, as it is when the harvest season is at its peak. The garden you've been dreaming of is in bloom! During this time, the main focus will be staying on top of harvesting. Enjoy this time and take a few simple steps to prepare for the end of the season.

☐ **Summer harvest:** With your flowers in full bloom, plan to harvest at least a few times per week. When harvesting, cut flowers in the cool morning hours, when they are crisp from the night dew.

☐ **Plant cool-season flowers:** Some fall plants, such as calendula and amaranth, are quick to germinate and bloom. If you have yet to plant cool-season flowers, there is still time to plant those with fewer days to maturity. Check your first frost date before planting to ensure that there is time left in your region's season.

☐ **Deadhead garden:** It is important to stay on top of deadheading any flowers you do not harvest to prevent your plants from going to seed. On your daily garden walk, take a pair of clippers and do a quick sweep-through of each garden bed, snipping off any past-their-prime blooms.

☐ **Pest prevention:** With the summer heat comes insect pests. Insects often hit their prime in the warmer weather, so staying on top of garden maintenance will reduce their presence in your garden. While deadheading and harvesting, make sure not to leave any compostable material lying around for bugs to nest in.

☐ **Save and preserve flowers:** Prepare a harvest for preservation! The late summer months are the perfect time to dry and press flowers to enjoy when the season is over.

Early Fall

As summer flowers begin to wind down, fall flowers will bloom through the first frost. The fall season is a busy time for gardeners who are wrapping up their cut flower season and preparing for the next one. It is a time of transition and a bittersweet end to the cycle.

☐ **Harvest cool-season flowers:** Flowers such as dahlias will be hitting their peak during the month of September. These flowers benefit from being cut and will reward you with more blooms up until the freezing temperatures. Gardeners enjoy fall bouquets filled with sunflowers, celosia, dahlias, and amaranth, often through October.

☐ **Seed collecting:** If you are interested in saving seeds from your flower season, now is the time. Let your plants flower without deadheading, and they will create seed. Wait until the plant is dead and dry, then harvest seed pods to save for your next season.

☐ **Overwinter garden beds:** The largest job in the fall for gardeners is preparing their garden beds for winter. Once you have collected seed or your flowers are winding down, plants can be cut back or dug up to clean out the bed. Consider covering beds with mulch or a cover crop to retain nutrients for your next growing season.

☐ **Plant spring bulbs:** Fall is the perfect time to tuck in your spring bulbs for early blooms. Tulips, hyacinth, and narcissus can all be planted in the fall and over-wintered. Ranunculus and anemones can also be started at this time; however, they may need more protection, such as a frost-cloth caterpillar tunnel.

☐ **Dig tubers:** If you grew dahlias and are planning on dividing tubers or the root stock, now is the time to dig. Dahlias produce new tubers throughout the season, and although it isn't necessary, you can divide them up and plant them as more plants in the spring. Find more information in the dahlia flower profile (page 146).

Winterizing and the End of the Growing Season

Winter is the season of rest for gardeners, but not before your garden is tucked in. Cleaning out and covering your garden are tasks that can be easily accomplished before the winter weather arrives. Preparing your flower beds now for the freezing temperatures and precipitation will guarantee healthy soil for next year's planting season.

☐ **Clean out the beds:** Before covering your flower beds for the winter season, dig out any annual flowers and weeds. Once dug, these materials can be composted. Any bulbs or tubers that you won't be leaving in the ground need to be dug up, and tubers can be divided. Although bulbs and tubers can be left in the ground for the next season, dig them up at least every other year so that they do not crowd one another.

☐ **Prepare the beds:** Once the beds are cleared, it is time to protect the soil for the winter. Flower bed soil can be topped with a cover crop, a plant that is seeded to protect the soil over the winter, but it will need to be pulled out before planting. A common cover crop is clover, as it adds nutrients back into the soil. Another option, instead of planting a cover crop, is mulching the top of your flower beds with 2 to 3 inches of leaf mold. This acts as a protective barrier so that the soil will not be washed away by rain or snow.

☐ **Plan your garden:** Winter is the time that many farms have their yearly seed, bulb, and tuber sales. During this time, plan what you would like to grow in your next flowering season, then purchase seeds. It is also the time to prepare your own collected seeds by separating the chaffs from the seeds, if previously harvested. Store in a cool, dry place until they are ready to plant in the new year.

FAQ: Garden Maintenance and Harvest

Still not sure if you're properly maintaining your garden? Read on for solutions to common maintenance problems.

Q: How much do I water my plants?

> **A:** Watering needs will vary depending on the plant variety and the season. Many gardeners will visually examine the soil and plant to see if they are hydrated. The soil should generally be moist, not just on top but a few inches down. You can also use a moisture meter in your soil to measure the amount of water in your soil and adjust from there. Be sure to water in the morning, before the heat of the day.

Q: What are my options for organic soil amendments?

> **A:** Choose your soil amendments based on your garden soil's pH balance. To increase the soil pH balance, add pulverized garden lime. To lower the pH, use an organic soil sulfur. If you are looking to add nitrogen to your garden soil, blood meal, chicken manure, or mushroom compost will add it naturally. To add phosphorus, try bat guano or bone meal. To add potassium, dig in kelp meal or langbeinite. Be sure to research what flowers do best with what feed before amending your soil.

Q: Do my flowers have a virus or disease?

A: Virus, disease, and fungus can unfortunately be common occurrences in the garden. Flowers may arrive diseased upon purchase, or the root stock may be infected. Either way, it can be near impossible to avoid. If you suspect a virus in your garden, don't panic. First, look for common signs of an infection. Yellowing on leaves (especially along the veins), leaf deformities or twisting, or target-like spots can all be indicators of disease. In many cases, the only way to confirm if it is a virus is to get the plant tested, but it is better to be safe than sorry! If you see a common disease pattern on your flowers, remove the infected plant before it can spread. Do not compost infected plants. Removing these plants, although disappointing, will ensure that the rest of your garden stays happy and healthy.

Q: What's a humane method of deterring rodents?

A: To deter rodents, first make sure that your plants or seedlings are protected with either a chicken wire cage or a low tunnel. Make sure that your garden area is clean and clutter-free, because rodents are often attracted to areas of clutter. Invest in live traps that can catch rodents, and then release them into the woods or a field, far away from your garden. You can also plant mint around your garden to act as a natural deterrent.

Q: How do I protect my garden from a storm?

A: Heavy rain, hail, and high winds can all cause damage to your garden. When extreme weather conditions are predicted, protect your garden with covers or barriers. Buckets, bins, and tubs can all be turned over to cover any smaller plants. Larger plants can be staked and covered with frost fabric or burlap to create a barrier. Small hoops, or even larger ones made with PVC piping, can act as protection for your garden when weather hits. If your plants do get damaged, cut off the damaged bits and they will likely try to regrow.

Q: When should I expect my first harvest?

A: All flowers have different times to maturity, so be sure to check the back of your seed packet before planting. Spring flowers such as tulips, narcissus, and hyacinth have a single flower harvest and often bloom mid-spring. Summer flowers such as zinnias and cosmos are "cut and come again" flowers, often blooming into the fall with milder temperatures. Summer flowers hit their peak season in July, with fall flowers such as dahlias and amaranth hitting their peak in September.

LILY [page 118]

6

Cutting and Arranging Beautiful Blooms

All your hard work, planning, and planting have paid off, and now it's time to enjoy your cut flowers! Once your garden is in bloom, it is time to focus on harvesting and arranging your blooms. A few key tips and tools will ensure that your flowers are cut in a way that prolongs their life in a vase and keeps them fresher longer. In this chapter, we will walk through how to properly cut, store, and arrange your flowers. From tools for harvesting to the key elements of a flower arrangement, find out what to do with your garden now that it is in bloom.

How to Harvest

Cutting your blooms is one of the most rewarding steps of the gardening process. It is important to keep on top of harvesting your flowers, so carve out time every day to walk to your garden and check what might need to be cut. When harvesting your flowers, cut them during the coolest parts of the day, preferably early morning, to keep them hydrated and fresh. Flowers picked midday are more likely to wilt and have a shorter vase life. Keep buckets of fresh, cool water at the ready to store cut stems in. Once the flowers are cut from the plant, they will need hydration right away—don't let them sit out for long without it.

Many flowering plants benefit from being cut deep into the plant rather than cutting a short stem. Don't be afraid to cut down past a leaf set. This will often encourage the plant to send out new growth, producing more flowers during the season. Once your flowers have been cut and placed into a bucket with water, let them rest in a cool place before use. Often garden flowers may have some lingering bugs on them, and letting them rest will allow those bugs to remove themselves prior to use. For the longest vase life, give flowers a fresh diagonal cut before placing them in a vase. There's no need to put additives in the water or crush the flower stems—a clean cut and fresh water will keep them happiest!

Getting More from Your Garden

After working so hard to bring your cut flower garden to life, you want your blooms to last in a vase for as long as possible. Storing your flowers properly is essential for keeping them at their freshest for the longest amount of time. Following a few simple harvesting and care tips will make this step easy.

Storing Your Flowers

Once cut, your flowers may need to be stored before arranging. In this case, keep your flowers hydrated in a bucket of water before use. Your bucket should be placed away from direct sunlight, as direct light could force the flowers to age faster than desired. Also keep your flowers in a cool room. It is unnecessary to keep blooms in the refrigerator, because it is often set too cold and will kill the delicate flowers. Instead, find a room in your house that maintains a cooler temperature. Flowers bloom in heat, so keeping them cool will keep the petal closed and encourage them to last longer prior to arranging.

Tools for Harvesting and Storing Flowers

Although you will be able to cut flowers from your garden with the essential tools provided at the beginning of this book (page 7), there are a few tools specifically for harvesting and arranging flowers that will help tremendously.

Clippers: A good pair of clippers or floral scissors is extremely helpful. Look for ones with a sharp, pointy tip—bonsai scissors work well for this.

Pruning shears: For cutting thicker stems, such as roses, use pruning shears. Fiskars is a reputable brand found at any garden center.

Buckets: Keep clean plastic buckets at the ready when harvesting flowers. These can be found at most stores; however, check with grocery store floral departments to see if they have any they are recycling. Often you can get some at no cost!

Jars or vases: When designing with florals, have vessels available for use. Look for vases that are about three times as tall as they are wide. Avoid long skinny vases with small openings when designing fuller arrangements.

Floral tape: Although not strictly necessary, floral tape can come in handy when designing to hold your flowers in a certain spot. Create a grid over the mouth of your vase with tape, and your stems will more easily stay where you want them to.

Extending the Life of Your Cut Flowers

The key to longevity in floral arrangements is fresh, clean water. Refresh your flowers' water daily and give the stems a fresh cut every few days. As the stems age, they begin to rot in the water. As soon as you see rot, remove that flower. Bacteria in the water will cut your vase life more than anything else. When arranging, also be sure to remove any leaves that would be submerged in the water, because they will rot first and invite bacteria.

Planning a Cut Flower Arrangement

Think of the most beautiful flower arrangement you have ever received. What made it beautiful? Maybe it was the unique mix of colors in the flower petals, or maybe it was a whimsical, unexpected texture. Perhaps it was because of how it smelled, or even who gave it to you. Flower arrangements can be special for so many reasons, and creating one can be a thoughtful, caring act. In order to create an impactful arrangement, it is important to keep color, size, shape, and texture in mind. Here I will share some of my favorite elements to consider when designing garden bouquets.

Color

Color is often the first thing noticed in an arrangement, so it is important to choose ones that bring you joy. Though there is no hard and fast rule when choosing hues, keep in mind color theory. Complementary colors are pleasing to the eye and add interest without chaos. For example, add a hint of light blue among a pink and orange bouquet for a fun and unique contrast.

Size

A balanced floral arrangement often includes a focal flower and supporting flowers. Focal flowers, such as roses, peonies, or dahlias, are the larger blooms used, whereas supporting blooms, such as zinnias, scabiosas, or strawflowers, are smaller and add variety and interest. Varying sizes break up the pattern to the eye, creating depth. When designing, try to also place your flowers of different sizes on different planes. For example, try not to place two flowers of the same size directly next to each other. Instead, place one near the center of the arrangement and pull one farther out.

Shape

Differ your shapes in flowers and foliage by choosing some that are long and pointy, some that are fuller and flat, and some that are more varied. Designers often use long and pointy flowers, or "spikes," to draw the eye upward in an arrangement. An example of spikes could be foxgloves or snapdragons. "Plates," or fuller, wider flowers, are included in arrangements to fill them out. Phlox and yarrow are perfect filler flowers.

Textural Elements

Add texture with organic matter like ornamental grasses, seed pods, or flower buds to elevate your floral arrangements. Diversity in your floral choices can create a unique, interesting combination that draws the eye through the arrangement. Experiment with different elements to see what works! Try adding flowers in different blooming stages or wild grasses and berries for a "wild garden" effect.

Personality

Your arrangements should reflect your love of flowers and your garden, so add some of your personality to it! Whimsical elements such as sweet pea tendrils or wispy cosmos add movement and motion. Think of your arrangements as an extension of your garden—how do your flowers grow? Don't be afraid to add airy, unique elements to make your arrangements your own.

Anatomy of an Arrangement

Applying some basic design principles will elevate both your bouquets (handheld wrapped designs) and your arrangements (vase designs). As a general guide, using the rule of thirds will create balance. For example, try using three focal flowers and arranging them in a triangular arrangement. Additionally, always create a floral arrangement that is size-appropriate for the vase selection. Again, using the rule of thirds, the flowers could be two-thirds of the total height with the vase being one-third. Add unique blooms at varied heights for a dynamic piece. Read on to learn more about the key elements that make up beautiful arrangements.

The Focal Flower

The focal flower of the arrangement is the flower that you want to highlight. They are often the centerpiece of the arrangement and can be on display toward the front of your design. To create balance, add focal flowers throughout the arrangement at varying heights and planes. Focal flowers are often larger blooms such as peonies, roses, lilies, dahlias, mums, and sunflowers. However, don't feel limited by those choices—any bloom that you want to celebrate can be a focal flower with the right placement. Experiment with different types of flowers and various colors to create a joyful, dynamic piece.

Secondary and Filler Flowers

Secondary and filler flowers play an important role in floral arranging. They are used to balance out the space and draw attention to the focal flowers. Secondary flowers are often smaller blooms compared to the focal flower; however, they are also intended to be highlighted. Complementary secondary flowers could include zinnias, ranunculus, tulips, strawflowers, scabiosas, asters, or even smaller versions of the focal flower. Set them lower in the arrangement or pull them out past the focal flower to create depth.

Filler flowers, or plates, fill any gaps in your arrangement and act as a base. They are great for filling holes during or after the arranging process. Example filler flowers could be sweet peas, yarrow, or phlox. These elements are often set low in the arrangement or at an even plane. For particularly wide and flat filler flowers such as yarrow, keep them snug in your arrangement rather than elevated above the other blooms.

Spikes and Airy Elements

To add height to your arrangements, design with tall and slender spike flowers. These blooms break any flat planes you may have and draw the eye up and out. Gladiola, snapdragon, stock, celosia, larkspur, or foxglove are all perfect spike elements. You can also elevate your arrangement by using elements that add a whimsical, airy effect. Sweet pea tendrils, cosmos, or ornamental grasses are all bouncy elements that add movement and playfulness to your arrangement. Don't be afraid to forage for these fun textures! Grasses make a perfect airy texture and can often be found around your neighborhood or on walks. Just be sure that whatever you cut isn't from someone else's garden!

Greenery

Foliage and greenery fill out any arrangement and create a fresh, full appearance. If you have a particularly leafy plant, such as peonies or tulips, use their greenery. Experiment with adding other greenery that you grew or foraged. For example, cress is wonderfully textural and easy to grow. Additionally, try using native greens in your arrangements that you can forage. In some regions, ferns and salal are plentiful, whereas in others you might have natural eucalyptus. Your greens can act as the base of your arrangement and can be placed first as the foundation to frame your other blooms.

FAQ: Flower Arranging

Here are some of the most common questions about creating beautiful flower arrangements.

Q: Flower foam or no flower foam?

A: Flower foam has been used as an easy way to keep stems stable when creating low or asymmetrical arrangements. I'm here to tell you: Ditch the foam. There are many just as simple ways to secure stems while also not negatively impacting the environment. Floral foam is made up of phenol-formaldehyde resin microplastics that not only contribute to environmental problems but are also toxic to humans. Instead, use a chicken wire base by cutting a piece of chicken wire that fits across the opening of the vessel and taping it in by stretching floral tape across the top of your vessel in an X pattern. You can also use flower frogs, which are weighted metal pin cushions that hold stems in place while designing. They can be used over and over again, and often can be found at your local thrift store.

Q: How do I make an arrangement look nice from every angle?

A: Beginning floral arrangements can often be one-sided or front facing, meaning that there is a definite front and the back looks bare. There is nothing wrong with this! However, if you are wanting to achieve a complete look from all angles, try designing on a lazy Susan. Place your vase on the lazy Susan and easily rotate the arrangement as you go. This will give you a 360-degree view of your progress and make it simple to create a lush, cohesive design.

Q: How do I help my stems stay in place?

A: Begin your design with the heaviest, woodiest stems to create a base. Your greenery, twigs, branches, or even roses can be the perfect materials to begin with in order to frame your arrangement. After you lay the foundation, these stems will act as a support structure for softer-stemmed flowers. Ultimately, the stems will begin to intertwine and weave together as you progress, holding one another up.

Q: What do I do when some flowers in the arrangement die?

A: As soon as you see spent flowers in your arrangement, pull them out. A mixed arrangement can include flowers that will all have different vase lives, and it's important to remove decaying material as it presents itself. For example, tulips have a much shorter vase life than ranunculus. If these two flowers are arranged together, the tulips should be removed as they die to prevent the bacteria from killing the ranunculus. This can be a fun way to change your arrangement as the days and weeks go by to get the most time out of it.

Q: How do I create a wrapped bouquet?

A: If you are planning on gifting a wrapped bouquet without a vase, follow these easy steps to create a full, dynamic bouquet: When arranging a bouquet, start with two sturdy stems and create an X shape with the stems. Lay in new stems to your handheld arrangement at a 45-degree angle to the previously added stems. This will create a fuller look instead of resulting in a straight-up-and-down bouquet. Adjust your hand as you add more stems, remembering to keep it loose so you don't squish the stems together. Keep rotating the arrangement so that flowers are added evenly. When finished, take a rubber band and loop it around the section of stems that you have been holding. This will keep your general arrangement shape. Snip the stems to the same length, wrap with a piece of paper, and finish off with a ribbon! This is a beautiful way to present your homegrown blooms to others.

SCABIOSA [page 128]

PART 2

Flower Profiles

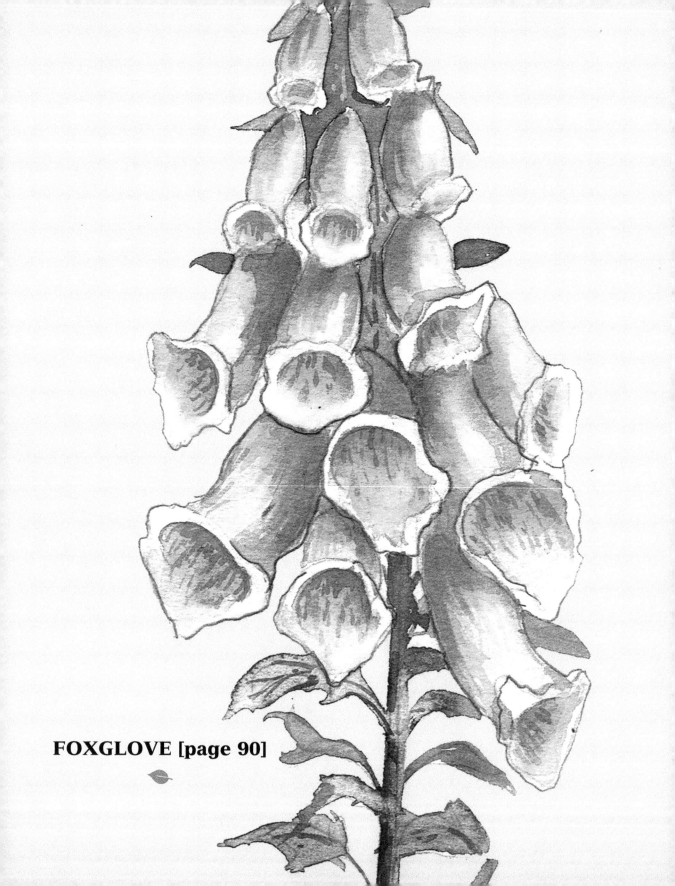

FOXGLOVE [page 90]

7

Spring Flowers

Anemone

Annual or perennial: Perennial

Latin name: *Anemone*

Family: Ranunculaceae

Growing zones: 3 to 10

Growing season: Spring

Start indoors or direct sow: Direct sow

Earliest planting: Zones 3 to 6 plant in the early spring, zones 7 to 10 plant in the fall and over winter

Sun needs: Full sun to partial shade

Water needs: Once plants are established, water to keep the soil consistently moist

Soil needs: Nutritious soil with ample compost and fertilizer

Suggested varieties for beginners: De Caen varieties of any color

Yield per plant: 20 to 30 flowers per corm

Troubleshooting tip: If temperatures drop below freezing, consider placing a layer of frost cloth on top of plants for protection.

Snapshot

- With their cupped, single layer of petals and open centers, anemones are a sweet, delicate display of color that blooms prolifically all spring. As a perennial, anemones are easy to grow and can be left in the soil of temperate zones to bloom the following year.

Starting

- In cooler zones, anemones should be planted in full sun. In more temperate climates, anemones can be planted in partial shade.
- Anemones are often direct sown, but they can also be pre-sprouted indoors. Soak corms for 4 hours in room temperature, aerated water. Once plump and hydrated, plant the corms directly in garden soil.
- If pre-sprouting, start corms in a shallow tray of moist seed-starting soil and keep in a cool, dark location, making sure it doesn't get too moist. After 2 weeks, roots should have sprouted, and these can be transplanted outdoors.
- If planting in zones 7 to 10, where you can plant anemones outdoors in the fall, be sure to cover your plants with a frost-cloth caterpillar tunnel if temperatures get close to freezing.

Growing

- Anemones benefit from moist soil. Water at ground level to keep the soil damp.
- Plant in compost-rich soil and consider adding a standard flower fertilizer to feed your new plants.

Harvesting

- Harvest when blooms are still in the bud stage. Cut the stem low and deep into the plant, and recut at an angle before placing them in water. Anemones harvested early will last 10 to 14 days in a vase of clean water.

Overwintering

- Because anemones grow from corms (which are similar to bulbs and look like dried acorns), you can leave these buried and attempt to regrow them the following season. This works best in temperate climates with fewer freezing temperatures. Although they can come back, many flower gardeners replant new corms yearly.

Common Problems

- Aphids and thrips are common anemone pests. When spotted, cut the affected section off or spray lightly with diluted soapy water. Aphids can also be easily squashed to prevent reproduction.

Bearded Iris

Annual or perennial: Perennial

Latin name: *Iris germanica*

Family: Iradaceae

Growing zones: 3 to 9

Growing season: Late spring

Start indoors or direct sow: Direct sow

Earliest planting: Fall

Sun needs: Full sun

Water needs: Susceptible to rot, do not overwater

Soil needs: Well-draining sandy loam

Suggested varieties for beginners: Beverly Sills, Country Kisses, Center Line

Yield per plant: One stem per rhizome and multiple flowers per stem

Fun fact: Iris fragrance oils come from the roots, not the flower!

Snapshot

- With their three large cascading petals, bearded irises are a wonderful perennial to add to your garden. They come in almost every color, and they multiply over the years, naturally expanding your flower garden.

Starting

- Plant in a location with at least 6 hours of sunlight, preferably full sun.
- Bearded irises need ample space to grow—plant blooms 18 to 24 inches apart. When seed pods form at the end of the season, remove to avoid overcrowding.
- Irises don't need mulching, as mulch can retain moisture that in turn can rot the rhizomes.
- Rhizomes, or the root stock of the plant, multiply yearly. Plan to dig up and divide the rhizomes once every 3 to 4 years.
- Plant bearded iris in well-draining soil and fertilize with low-nitrogen, high-phosphate fertilizer. Amend with bone meal and ensure that soil is loose enough to expel any excess moisture while maintaining dampness to the touch.

Growing

- Irises need less frequent watering than most flowering plants. Water is needed at first planting before the roots take hold. Avoid watering over the winter, and then provide a deep water at the beginning of spring. It is recommended to do less frequent, deep watering rather than frequent, shallow watering.
- Ensure that the top of the rhizomes is exposed to the light and elements. Prune any browning leaves down to the base, leaving the healthy green leaves through the summer.

Harvesting and Drying

- Bearded iris stalks have multiple blooms per stem with staggered blooming times. Cut when the top flower is in bloom and the subsequent flowers are buds; flowers will continue to open after cutting. Remove the spent top flowers after blooming is done.

Seed Saving

- Flowers will turn to seed pods after blooming. Remove the seed pods from the plant before self-seeding. Multiply flower stock by dividing the rhizomes.

Common Problems

- Irises are susceptible to overwatering and rot. If rhizomes are becoming soft, attempt to plant in a raised bed or a slightly sloped ground to help the soil drain.

Daffodil

Annual or perennial: Perennial

Latin name: *Narcissus pseudonarcissus*

Family: Amaryllidaceae

Growing zones: 3 to 9

Growing season: Early spring

Start indoors or direct sow: Direct sow

Earliest planting: Fall

Sun needs: Full to partial sun

Water needs: Water in dry spring weather

Soil needs: Well-draining, neutral to acidic soil

Suggested varieties for beginners: Pink Charm, Orangery, Petit Four

Yield per plant: 1 to 3 flowers per bulb

Keep in mind tip: There are many different types of daffodils besides the classic yellow! Daffodils can be white, cream, yellow, peach, and orange, and they come in many different shapes and sizes.

Snapshot

- These dainty, cheerful blossoms are a sure sign that spring has arrived. Often one of the first flowers to bloom, daffodil's trumpet-shaped centers and petticoat of petals are a beautiful addition to any garden.

Starting

- Plant daffodils in full sun to partial shade in well-draining soil.
- Bulbs need to be planted point side up, 5 inches deep with 3 to 4 inches of spacing between plants.
- Bulbs can be dug up and moved in the fall. Over the year, smaller bulbs will form off the main bulb, creating a small patch of blooms.
- Plant in the fall 3 to 4 weeks before the first frost.

Growing

- Water plants deeply in the spring, taking care not to overwater.
- After the first season, add bone meal to the soil surrounding the plant to encourage growth the following year.

Harvesting and Arranging

- Cut daffodils when they are fully in bloom. Make sure to cut low, down at the base of the plant, not only to get the longest stem possible but also to cut down the plant.
- Although they do not dry well on their own, daffodils can be preserved using silica gel.
- Daffodils do best as a single-flower arrangement. This is because the sap that secretes from the stem after cutting is known to speed up the rotting process for other flower types. If using in a mixed arrangement, soak stems on their own prior to designing.

Seed Saving

- Although you can save seed from daffodils after the flower has dried on the plant, seed-starting daffodils will take 5 to 7 years to bloom. Home gardeners typically use bulbs purchased in the spring as the main method of growing daffodils.

Common Problems

- Daffodil bulbs can sometimes disappear at the hands of rodents. To protect your bulbs over winter, use chicken wire cages or blood meal to keep unwanted pests away.

Foxglove

Annual or perennial: Biennial

Latin name: *Digitalis*

Family: Plantaginaceae

Growing zones: 4 to 10

Growing season: Late spring

Start indoors or direct sow: Start indoors and transplant after the last frost

Indoor sowing date: 10 to 12 weeks prior to the last frost date

Earliest planting: Late summer

Sun needs: Full sun with afternoon shade

Water needs: Keep the soil moist without drying out or overwatering

Soil needs: Rich soil with compost

Suggested varieties for beginners: Camelot White, Dalmatian Peach, Candy Mountain

Yield per plant: One spike per season

Fun fact: Modern medicine uses compounds found in foxgloves to treat heart failure.

Snapshot

- With their spike of colorful blooms, foxgloves have a "wild garden" appearance. Oftentimes growing 3 to 5 feet tall, they add impressive height to garden beds and floral arrangements.

Starting

- Foxgloves benefit from some afternoon shade. Plant in well-draining soil that will stay moist during the growing season.

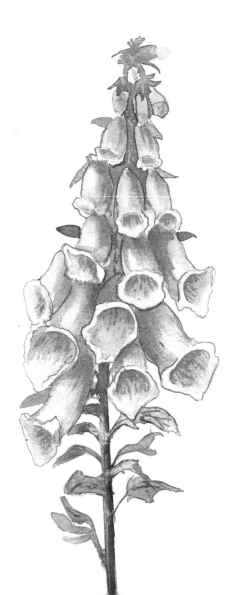

- Sow seeds indoors 10 to 12 weeks before your region's last frost date. Seeds need light to germinate and should be left uncovered by soil. As plants grow, transplant into larger containers to ensure the plants have space to grow before planting outside.
- When planting your established plants, harden them off after the last frost.

Growing

- Foxgloves need moist soil to flourish throughout the season. Water early in the morning. Avoid under- or overwatering, which stunts the growth of the plant.
- As a biennial, foxgloves put off foliage the first year, then bloom the second year before dying. Plant foxgloves 2 years in a row for more continual blooms with reseeding.
- Since foxgloves are tall plants, be prepared to stake your blooms during the season. Use a plastic or bamboo stake with twine for easy stabilization.

Harvesting

- To harvest, cut the flower spike low at the base of the plant. Although technically the plant produces one flower per season, cutting low will encourage the plant to potentially put off more blooms. Keep in mind that foxgloves are poisonous to humans and animals. Keep out of the reach of children and pets.

Seed Saving

- Foxgloves are generally known as self-seeders, meaning they will drop their seeds at the end of the season. When the dropped seeds sprout, thin out the successful seedlings to avoid overcrowding. Plants will flower every other year.

Common Problems

- Powdery mildew can be a common problem with foxgloves in warm, humid, shady, and damp conditions. To avoid this, plant foxgloves in a location that receives at least 6 hours of sunlight. If plants become affected, clip off mildewed leaves and sanitize the clippers between plants.

Hyacinth

Annual or perennial: Perennial

Latin name: *Hyacinthus*

Family: Asparagaceae

Growing zones: 3 to 9

Growing season: Mid-spring

Start indoors or direct sow: Direct sow

Earliest planting: Mid- to late fall

Sun needs: Full to partial sun

Water needs: Water when the soil becomes dry, highly susceptible to overwatering

Soil needs: Loosened, loamy soil

Suggested varieties for beginners: Dutch hyacinths: Gipsy Queen, Splendid Cornelia, Miss Saigon

Yield per plant: One flower per bulb

Keep in mind tip: Hyacinth bulbs can be forced to start indoors. Plant in a pot with drainage and keep in a dark, cool place until the bulb has sprouted. Once above soil, gradually increase light and watering until it is time to transplant in the spring.

Snapshot

- One of the most beautifully fragranced flowers, hyacinth is a spring staple to grow in your yard or garden. Though the stems are on the shorter side, the flowers add a springtime elegance to your outdoor landscaping or floral arrangements.

Starting

- Plant bulbs in well-draining, loosened soil in a sunny location. Bulbs need to be planted with the pointy side facing up, 5 to 6 inches deep. When planting multiple bulbs, space 6 to 7 inches apart.

- If you force bulbs to start indoors, it is best to transplant outdoors in late fall; however, you can also plant them outside in early spring.
- Be aware that bulbs contain an element that is toxic to pets and can be harmful to bare skin. Be sure to wear gloves when planting and keep away from pets.

Growing

- When watering, be sure to water at the base of the plant rather than overhead. If planting in a region that gets a lot of rainfall, consider planting in containers that can be covered.
- When planting, use mulch and compost to add necessary nutrients into the soil. Mulch will also help prevent weeds throughout the season.

Harvesting

- When harvesting hyacinths, wait until the flower has bloomed. Cut the flower stem down to the base, leaving the foliage attached. Once cut, keep in cool water for the longest vase life. Stems are known to be weak; if bending, reinforce by sticking floral wire through the stem to add support.

Overwintering

- If planted in the right conditions and well maintained, hyacinth bulbs can rebloom the following season. Let the leaves die on the plant to help nourish it, and cut back dead foliage after winter.

Common Problems

- Because hyacinths are prone to overwatering, gray mold and rotting can be common problems. To avoid, use a drip system or carefully water the ground around the plant.

Peony

Annual or perennial: Perennial

Latin name: *Paeonia*

Family: Paeoniaceae

Growing zones: 3 to 8

Growing season: Late spring, early summer

Start indoors or direct sow: Direct sow

Earliest planting: Early fall

Sun needs: 6 to 8 hours of sunlight

Water needs: Drought-tolerant, but benefits from consistent water weekly to keep the soil moist

Soil needs: Well-draining, deep, nutritious soil with a neutral pH

Suggested varieties for beginners: Coral Charm, Moonstone, Anna Marie

Yield per plant: Peonies develop a larger flower yield as they age. They often do not bloom the first year, but in the second year you can expect 5 to 7 blooms. By the fifth year, plants can put off 20 to 30 flowers per season.

Fun fact: Peony petals are edible! Try them in a jelly or your favorite drink.

Snapshot

- Peonies are often described as the queens of the flower garden, with their large, ruffly, prolific blooms. Plants come in a variety of shapes and colors, many of which have a sweet, roselike scent. Although they take at least a year to bloom, the wait is worthwhile.

Starting

- Peonies do best planted in deep, well-draining soil with full to partial sun. When planting, choose a location that can be permanent, because peonies resent transplant. Plants grow large over the years, so establish an area free of other plants that the peonies would have to compete with.

- Peony plants often come as "bare root," meaning they come with their roots cleared of soil and ready for planting rather than starting from seed. To plant, dig a large hole and amend with compost and bone meal. Place the roots in the hole with the sprouts, or "eyes," facing upward. Cover with soil and compost so that the sprouts are only 2 inches below the surface.

Growing

- Peonies benefit from deep watering weekly to keep the soil moist.
- Peonies produce beautiful, large blooms that can cause the stems to bend and tip. Stake the plant and grow in a protected area to prevent wind damage.

Harvesting

- When harvesting, cut the blooms when they are still in the bud stage. Gently squeeze the buds between your fingers—if they are hard like a marble, they are not ready; if they are squishy like a marshmallow, they are ready to be cut.

Common Problems

- Japanese beetles are a common pest found on peonies. An easy fix is to put an organza bag over the blooms to protect them from the beetles. To treat them, set traps around your blooms or plant geraniums nearby so they can attract the beetles instead. However, a natural chemical found in the leaves of geranium causes them to fall off the plant and die.

Poppy

Annual or perennial: Hardy annual

Latin name: *Papaver*

Family: Papaveraceae

Growing zones: 3 to 11

Growing season: Late spring to
early summer

Start indoors or direct sow:
Direct sow

Indoor sowing date: Plant 6 to 8 weeks
before planting outside under cover

Earliest planting: Fall or early spring

Sun needs: Direct sun

Water needs: Water to keep the soil moist

Soil needs: Well-draining

Suggested varieties for beginners: Breadseed,
Shirley, Icelandic

Yield per plant: Cut and come again

Fun fact: Poppies were found in the tomb of
Tutankhamun, who was buried in 1325 BCE.

Snapshot

- These delicate, paperlike blooms create a spot of color in your garden and dance in the wind. Poppies are prolific bloomers and will provide you with handfuls of blooms all season long. Even after blooming, their pods make for a unique, desirable texture in floral arrangements.

Starting

- Poppies do best when planted in full sun to partial shade in well-draining, loamy soil. They tend to do well in raised beds. Plant in a well-protected area, because they can be susceptible to wind damage.

- Poppies can be started indoors; however, they resent transplanting. They do best by direct sowing in the early spring just prior to the last frost or in the late fall. If planting in the late fall, consider covering your bed with frost cloth to protect the young seedlings from the elements.
- Prepare soil for planting by removing any weeds, digging in organic compost, and raking the beds level. Mist the ground before planting, and then scatter the seeds on top of the soil without covering.

Growing

- Water plants every few days as needed. Keep the ground somewhat moist, but be cautious not to overwater. During warmer weather, water daily.
- If you plan to grow poppies as annuals, deadhead your flowers to prevent them from going to seed. Deadheading will also encourage plants to produce more flowers throughout the season.

Harvesting

- When harvesting, cut just as the petals are starting to emerge from the pod casing. Poppies are known for having a short vase life, so cutting them at this early stage will increase it.
- Poppies don't dry well, but once the flower is spent and the pod has emerged, cut it and hang it to dry for a unique texture.

Seed Saving

- Poppies can produce thousands of seeds from one plant. To collect, don't deadhead; instead, let your flowers go to seed. Once the pods have dried completely on the plant, cut the stems. Poke a hole in the seed head and dump out seeds into a paper envelope.

Common Problems

- If your plants aren't putting off many blooms, check the nitrogen levels in your soil. If the nitrogen is too high, it can lead to leaf growth instead of blooms. Condition with a phosphorus fertilizer to improve bloom output.

Ranunculus

Annual or perennial: Cool-season perennial

Latin name: *Ranunculus*

Family: Ranunculaceae

Growing zones: 3 to 10

Growing season: Mid- to late spring

Start indoors or direct sow: Direct sow or pre-sprout

Earliest planting: Fall or early spring

Sun needs: Full sun to afternoon shade

Water needs: Water deeply, not too frequently

Soil needs: Loamy, well-draining soil

Suggested varieties for beginners: Marshmallow, White Picotee, Salmon

Yield per plant: 20 to 30 blooms per corm

Troubleshooting tip: If ranunculus are planted in the fall, be careful of freezing temperatures. Ranunculus can be affected by frostbite if the temperatures dip below freezing, so to protect them, cover them with a frost-cloth, low tunnel, or caterpillar tunnel.

Snapshot

- Ranunculus are a showstopper in flower gardens; their soft, romantic, ruffly blooms continually sprout all season. They are popular in flower designs, due to their beautiful colors and extremely long vase life as a cut flower.

Starting

- Ranunculus are susceptible to freezing temperatures and overwatering, so plant them in a location with full sun and well-draining water. Raised beds or containers are great locations to grow these flowers.

- Before planting, soak your corms in room temperature water for around 4 hours to rehydrate. Once plump, they can be planted outside or pre-sprouted.
- If pre-sprouting indoors, transplant outside in the fall or spring, depending on your zone, and cover plants with frost cloth to protect them from frost.
- When directly sowing corms, plant corms "tentacle"-side down, 2 inches under soil. Space them 6 to 9 inches apart.

Growing

- Ranunculus corms are easily overwatered, so water deeply less frequently to keep the soil moist.
- Soil should be mixed with compost for maximum nutrition and fertilized as needed. When planting in the cooler months, be prepared with hoops or caterpillar tunnels with frost cloth to protect against freezing temperatures.

Harvesting

- When harvesting ranunculus, cut flowers when the bud feels soft throughout when gently squeezed (also knows as the soft bud stage). When ready, cut the stem down to the base of the plant. Ranunculus are known to have an exceptionally long stem life. Cut flowers can last upwards of 2 weeks if kept in fresh, clean water.

Overwintering

- Technically, ranunculus are considered a perennial because they can return in following seasons in temperate climates. However, because ranunculus easily rot, many gardeners do not count on them returning and instead treat the flower as an annual.

Common Problems

- If your ranunculus leaves are turning yellow and wilting, it may be a lack of nitrogen or overwatering. If nitrogen levels are low, fertilize to restore. Adjust water levels if needed.

Sweet Pea

Annual or perennial: Annual

Latin name: *Lathyrus odoratus*

Family: Fabaceae

Growing zones: 2 to 11

Growing season: Spring

Start indoors or direct sow: Indoor sowing recommended

Indoor sowing date: Plant 2 weeks prior to transplant date

Earliest planting: Direct sow 5 to 6 weeks prior to the last frost date, when the soil can be worked

Sun needs: Full sun to partial afternoon shade

Water needs: Water when the soil becomes dry

Soil needs: Well-draining, neutral to slightly alkaline

Suggested varieties for beginners: April in Paris

Yield per plant: Blooms abundantly all season

Fun fact: Sweet peas grow extremely quickly and can climb up to 12 inches per week!

Snapshot

- A garden favorite, sweet peas provide delicate, sweet-smelling blooms throughout the spring. Their vines add vertical growth to any garden, making them a favorite cut flower of many home gardeners.

Starting

- Sweet peas do well in full sun to partial afternoon shade.
- Starting indoors and planting 5 to 6 weeks before the last frost date is recommended. Wait until the soil can be worked. When starting indoors, soak the seeds overnight to soften the shell and speed up the germination process. Plant seeds by poking a ½-inch hole in the soil and covering. Seeds will germinate in 10 to 14 days.
- Sweet peas can handle a light frost and should be planted outside 5 to 6 weeks prior to the last frost.

- Plant sweet peas 6 to 8 inches apart with room for the shoots to climb. When shoots have developed multiple leaf sets, pinch two leaf sets to encourage the plant to branch.

Growing

- Keep the soil moist by watering consistently at the base of the plant.
- Mix compost into the soil prior to planting. As the plant grows, keep the shoots tied to the trellis using twine to encourage upward growth.

Harvesting and Drying

- To ensure the longest vase life, cut the flowers with a few unopened buds on each stem. Keep the stems in fresh water and enjoy them for 5 days.
- Cut or deadhead your sweet peas often to prolong the blooming stage of your plant.
- Although they don't dry well, sweet peas make beautiful pressed flowers.

Seed Saving

- When the flowers are not cut, a seed pod will form. Continually cut flowers to prolong the blooming stage of your plant.
- Wait until the seed pods have completely dried out on your plant to pick and collect seeds. Collecting green pods will result in underdeveloped seeds.

Common Problems

- Aphids like to snack on sweet pea tendrils. When spotted, cut off the affected section of the plant or spray lightly with diluted soapy water. Aphids can also be easily squashed to prevent reproduction.

Tulip

Annual or perennial: Perennial

Latin name: *Tulipa*

Family: Liliaceae

Growing zones: 3 to 8

Growing season: Spring

Start indoors or direct sow: Direct sow

Earliest planting: Fall before the first frost

Sun needs: Full sun to partial afternoon shade

Water needs: Water at planting, and then not again until spring; water only when the soil is dry

Soil needs: Dry, sandy, well-draining soil

Suggested varieties for beginners: Angelique, Negrita, Menton

Yield per plant: One flower per bulb

Troubleshooting tip: If you unpacked your bulbs and found some mold on them, it may not be the time to panic. First, check the density of the bulbs. If the bulb is squishy to the touch, toss it. If it is still plump, plant it and it may still grow.

Snapshot

- The excitement of seeing the first tulip leaves poking out of the ground is a highlight for any gardener. This springtime staple blooms early and makes for a beautiful, elegant, and simple arrangement if gathered together. Tulips also come in almost every color, so there is a variety for everyone.

Starting

- When preparing beds, choose a location safe from excessive heat and with well-draining soil. Prepare the soil by loosening and adding fresh compost.
- When planting, place bulbs pointy side up, four times as deep as the bulb is tall. Bulbs can handle being planted close together, but 4 to 5 inches between bulbs is best.
- Once covered with soil, gently water to wake up the bulbs.

Growing

- Tulips do not need constant watering; in fact, this can easily rot the bulb. Water deeply when the soil is dry to the touch, 1 to 2 inches deep.
- Mix compost into the soil prior to planting. When leaves sprout in the spring, feed plants with fertilizer or bone meal.

Harvesting

- To harvest, wait for the flowers to be colorful but not fully opened. Snip the stem at the base of the plant. If growing as an annual, tulips can be fully pulled up by the bulb since the bulb will only produce one flower. If growing as a perennial, snip down stems but leave the foliage. Let the leaves die on the plant to provide the bulb with the nutrients needed, and then trim back.

Overwintering

- Tulips are considered a perennial; however, flowers left in the garden beds often will not produce stems as long or quality cut flowers the following years. If overwintering, fertilize with bone meal upon planting, and after the season before winter. Make sure the soil drains well over the winter to prevent bulb rot.

Common Problems

- Slugs can be a common pest for tulips. If left untreated, slugs can munch leaves down to the base. To deter, sprinkle Sluggo Plus or diatomaceous earth at the base of your plants.

LOVE-IN-A-MIST [page 120]

8

Summer Flowers

Bachelor's Button

Annual or perennial: Biannual

Latin name: *Centaurea cyanus*

Family: Asteraceae

Growing zones: 2 to 11

Growing season: Late spring to midsummer

Start indoors or direct sow: Direct sow recommended

Earliest planting: Late winter to early spring

Sun needs: Full sun to partial shade

Water needs: 1 inch of water per week

Soil needs: Sandy loam

Suggested varieties for beginners: Florist Blue Boy, Classic Magic

Yield per plant: Cut and come again

Fun fact: Bachelor's button blooms are edible! Use them to add unique color to salads, liven up your favorite cocktail, or spruce up the decor on cakes.

Snapshot

- Bachelor's buttons, or cornflower, are warm-season blooms that add pops of color to any garden. Their long stems and unique shades of blue, purple, and pink make them excellent cut flowers—or you can plant them as a pollinator crop in a vegetable garden.

Starting

- Find a location that has full sun to partial afternoon shade. In the warmer zones, plant bachelor's buttons with more afternoon shade to keep them blooming longer.
- Direct sow seeds in late winter. Seeds can withstand a light frost and will germinate in 10 to 14 days in nonfreezing temperatures. In cooler climates, plant in early spring. Plant seeds 6 to 9 inches apart and cover with ½ inch of soil. Keep the soil moist during the germination process.
- If desired, seeds can be sown indoors 3 to 4 weeks before the final frost. Harden off seedlings when multiple sets of leaves form. Plant in moist, composted soil after the last frost.

Growing

- Bachelor's buttons need around an inch of water per week, meaning the top inch of the soil stays moist. This is usually accomplished by 30 minutes of watering three times a week.
- As plants grow, use stakes to keep them upright.

Harvesting and Drying

- Keep on top of harvesting and deadheading to promote flower growth. When harvesting, cut low into the plant when the blooms are half-open.
- Bachelor's buttons make beautiful dried flowers, as they retain their colors. After harvesting, hang upside down in a cool, dry location for 2 weeks.

Seed Saving

- To collect seeds, let the flower dry out completely on the plant. Seeds can be found in the center of the bloom; gently flake them into your palm and place in a paper envelope to save for the next season.

Common Problems

- Bachelor's buttons are low-fuss, but can be susceptible to overwatering and aphids. Check your plants daily for stunted growth and adjust water levels if needed.

Calendula

Annual or perennial: Annual/short-lived perennial

Latin name: *Calendula officinalis*

Family: Asteraceae

Growing zones: 3 to 10

Growing season: Early summer to early fall

Start indoors or direct sow: Direct sow recommended

Earliest planting: After last frost

Sun needs: Full sun to partial shade

Water needs: 1½ inches of water weekly

Soil needs: Well-draining, neutral pH

Suggested varieties for beginners: Bronze Beauty, Ivory Princess, Orange Button

Yield per plant: Cut and come again

Fun fact: Calendula can be grown in your cut flower or herb garden. The plant has many medicinal benefits, such as antifungal, antioxidant, and anti-inflammatory properties that are often used to soothe rashes and eczema.

Snapshot

- Although relatively short, calendula is a lush, full bloom to grow in your garden. When full-grown, it somewhat resembles a daisy, and it comes in yellows, browns, and oranges. The flowers are extremely long-lasting and make rich, textural dried arrangements.

Starting

- Consider growing in a container or raised flower bed. Choose a location that has full sun to partial shade with well-draining soil.
- Direct sow seeds after the last frost, 6 inches apart and ¼ inch into the soil. Keep the soil moist during germination. Seeds usually germinate in 10 to 14 days.
- If desired, you can start them indoors, sowing seeds 4 to 5 weeks before the final frost. Harden off seedlings when they have multiple leaf sets and then transplant outside.
- To keep calendula flowers blooming through to the first frost, consider succession planting them. When succession planting, sow seeds staggered by a few weeks to have blooms in multiple stages.

Growing

- Calendula should only be watered when the surrounding soil feels dry to the touch. They benefit from compost added to the soil upon planting but are relatively low maintenance during the growing season.

Harvesting and Drying

- For arrangements, cut the blooms when they are about half-open. For medicinal properties or drying, cut when the bloom is fully opened. To dry, cut the blooms and hang upside down in a cool, dry location for 2 weeks.

Seed Saving

- If left to seed, calendulas can reseed themselves. To collect the seeds, let the blossoms dry out completely on the plant. Once dry, gently run your fingers over the flower head while collecting the seeds in a bag below. Store in a cool, dry location to be planted next season.

Common Problems

- If you notice your calendula plant dying, it could be due to warm weather. Cut back the stems and water well for the blooms to return again in the fall.

Cosmos

Annual or perennial: Annual

Latin name: *Cosmos bipinnatus*

Family: Asteraceae

Growing zones: 2 to 11

Growing season: Summer

Start indoors or direct sow: Start indoors

Earliest planting: 5 to 7 weeks before the last frost

Sun needs: Full sun

Water needs: 1 inch weekly

Soil needs: Neutral to alkaline, well-draining

Suggested varieties for beginners: Xsenia, Cupcake Blush, Afternoon White

Yield per plant: Cut and come again

Troubleshooting tip: If your cosmos seedlings are growing tall and leggy, make sure they are getting enough light. These seedlings grow quickly and need to be pinched to maintain a healthy, bushy plant.

Snapshot

- Cosmos are a distant relative of daisies, which is apparent in their delicate single layer of petals and open centers. These garden staples grow into large, bushy plants with ample blooms all season. They provide a light, frilly texture and will attract plenty of pollinators.

Starting

- Find a location with full sun and some wind protection. Soil should be regular to well-draining.
- Start seeds indoors 5 to 7 weeks prior to the last frost. Sow seeds in a 72-cell seed tray, keeping them well-lit and watered.
- After the frost, harden off seeds outdoors and plant 9 to 12 inches apart. Once seedlings have multiple leaf sets, pinch to encourage lateral growth.

Growing

- Cosmos can tolerate some soil dryness, but keep the soil watered between dry spells. Overwatering can result in fewer flowers. Drip irrigation is a great way to water cosmos, because when they are full-grown, they are large and more difficult to water at the base.
- Use stakes or corrals to keep plants upright. Stake the corners of your flower bed and string twine in between the stakes.

Harvesting

- Cosmos benefit from frequent cutting and deadheading. To extend their shorter vase life, cut when the blooms are just slightly open.

Seed Saving

- Cosmos are wonderful self-seeders. To collect seeds, let the flowers on the plant dry out completely, then gently pinch off the long seeds in the center of the blooms. Store in a cool, dry location until the following season.

Common Problems

- If you notice that your cosmos' leaves and stems are discolored and your plants are stunted or dying, they may have a fungal infection. Fusarium wilt (a common plant disease brought on by excess moisture and heat, causing leaves to wilt and die) can be common; if spotted, pull out the plants from the root and dispose. Avoid planting in that area until the soil can be replaced.

Gladiolus

Annual or perennial: Perennial

Latin name: *Gladiolus*

Family: Iridaceae

Growing zones: 7 to 10

Growing season: June to first frost

Start indoors or direct sow: Direct sow

Earliest planting: Early spring, 2 weeks before last frost

Sun needs: Full sun

Water needs: Water upon planting, and then weekly after sprouting

Soil needs: Sandy loam

Suggested varieties for beginners: Sugar Babe, White Prosperity, Black Pearl

Yield per plant: 1 to 3 stems of blooms

Keep in mind tip: Gladiolus are toxic to humans and pets. If ingested, they can cause nausea, diarrhea, or lethargy, so be sure to plant them somewhere that cannot be accessed by children or pets.

Snapshot

- These magnificent blooms bring a burst of color and drama to any garden. Gladiolus grow to be 2 to 5 feet tall and bloom in spikes, making for a stunning vertical element in cut flower gardens and arrangements. Flowers come in almost every color (except true blue) and have a long vase life.

Starting

- Gladiolus do best in full sun and take up minimal garden space. They can be planted in containers, raised beds, or directly into the ground. Choose a location that has well-draining, sandy loam soil.
- Just after the last frost, prepare the corms for planting (see page 85). Plant the corms 4 inches deep and spaced 3 to 5 inches apart. Once covered, give them deep water to begin the growing process.

Growing

- After the first water post-planting, do not water again until the plant has sprouted a few inches aboveground to avoid bulb rot. Once grown, water gladiolus weekly.
- Because gladiolus are tall plants, they may need to be staked. Close planting also helps the stems prop one another up.

Harvesting

- Since each corm usually only grows one stem, cut the stem down to the base when harvesting. Gladiolus have multiple blooms per stem that blossom at staggered times. Blooms will continue to open when cut and placed in water.

Overwintering

- Gladiolus do best when overwintered in zones 8 and above, where freezing temperatures are less frequent. In cooler zones, dig up the bulbs, let the corms fully dry out, then store in a cool, dry place until the following spring.

Common Problems

- Thrips can be a common pest for gladioli. Although they can be difficult to spot, look for twisting of leaves, discoloration, and stunted growth. To get rid of thrips, place sticky-tape thrip traps in the garden or release ladybugs on the affected plants to eat the pests.

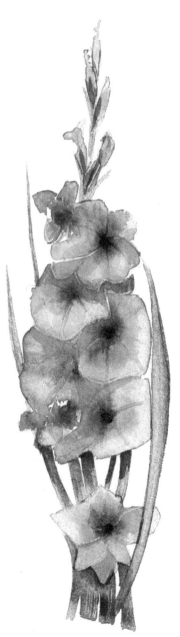

Hollyhock

Annual or perennial: Biennial/short-lived perennial

Latin name: *Alcea rosea*

Family: Malvaceae

Growing zones: 3 to 9

Growing season: Midsummer to fall

Start indoors or direct sow: Direct sow recommended

Earliest planting: Spring, after the last frost

Sun needs: Full sun

Water needs: 1 inch of water weekly

Soil needs: Well-draining, rich soil

Suggested varieties for beginners: Halo Blush, Double Apricot

Yield per plant: One large stalk, with multiple blooming offshoots

Fun fact: Although grown in very different climates, hollyhock flowers are related to hibiscus. They both have stunning, trumpet-shaped flowers and vibrant colors.

Snapshot

- The tall, flowered stalks of the hollyhock are a quintessential element of classic English gardens. The blooms can grow up to 6 feet tall and are adorned with blossoms up and down the stems. Whether they're pink, peach, burgundy, or purple, hollyhocks are a showstopping addition to any garden.

Starting

- Hollyhocks grow best when planted in rich, well-draining soil in full sun. Because of their height, they are well placed against a fence or toward the back of your garden beds.
- Direct sow outside after the last frost in late spring or early summer. Plant seeds ¼ inch into the soil and space plants 1½ to 2 feet apart.
- If desired, you can start hollyhocks indoors 6 to 8 weeks before transplanting outdoors.

Growing

- Make sure that the soil is moist during germination. After sprouting, water hollyhocks with 1 inch of water weekly.
- If not against a fence, add a trellis or other support for hollyhocks to grow into.

Harvesting

- Harvest hollyhock stems when one-third of their flowers are in bloom. Flowers will continue to open once cut and placed in fresh water.

Seed Saving

- Hollyhocks easily reseed themselves if the flowers die on the plant and drop seeds. Once seedlings come up, thin out extras to ensure they have enough room to grow.
- If you'd like to save the seeds, let flowers dry out completely on the plant. Once dry, pinch off the seeds and save in a cool, dry place until the following growing season.

Common Problems

- Hollyhock foliage is susceptible to rust on leaves—brown or orange spots on stems and foliage. To avoid rust, do not water the plants overhead. Instead, water at ground level or use a drip irrigation system. Also be sure to use correct spacing between plants. Ample spacing will encourage airflow that will also reduce the chances of rust.

Larkspur

Annual or perennial: Annual

Latin name: *Delphinium*

Family: Ranunculaceae

Growing zones: 2 to 10

Growing season: Summer

Start indoors or direct sow: Direct sow recommended

Earliest planting: Early spring or fall planting for overwintering

Sun needs: Direct sun

Water needs: 1 inch of water weekly

Soil needs: Well-composted, slightly alkaline, well-draining soil

Suggested varieties for beginners: Fancy Pink, Smokey Eyes, Earl Grey

Yield per plant: Multiple stems

Keep in mind tip: Larkspur seeds are unusual and need to go through a process of "scarification" to germinate and grow. This is when the hardened outer shell of the seed is exposed to cold and moisture to soften it and allow for germination.

Snapshot

- These tall, packed blooms are a beautiful addition to any cut flower garden. Larkspur are cold-hardy and produce multiple blooming stems throughout their growing season. They come in special colors, like smoky lavender, that add an elegant touch to cut flower arrangements.

Starting

- Choose a location with well-draining soil in full sun. In-ground garden beds or raised beds work perfectly.
- Direct sowing in the fall is recommended. Seeds will withstand the coldest temperatures and will germinate and flower in the late spring/early summer. Seeds can also be planted outside in the late winter/early spring. Plant seeds ¼ inch deep in soil and space 6 inches apart.
- If desired, larkspur seeds can be started indoors and transplanted outside. Start seeds 6 to 8 weeks before the last frost and plant outside while the weather is still cold.

Growing

- Keep the soil moist but water plants consistently. One inch of water weekly at ground level is recommended.
- Fertilize with a general 10-10-10 mix, if needed.

Harvesting and Drying

- For arrangements, harvest when one-third of the flowers are blooming. For drying, cut when there are only a few unopened flowers at the top. Hang the larkspur upside down in a cool, dry place away from any light for 2 weeks. The larkspur should retain its color. Note that this plant is poisonous, so keep out of the reach of children and pets.

Seed Saving

- Larkspur often self-seeds if flowers are left to die on the plant. To collect seeds, wait for the flowers to dry out completely and seed pods to form where the flowers were. Collect the pods and store them in a cool, dry location to be planted the next season.

Common Problems

- If your larkspur is drooping and has yellowing leaves, it could be that it is overwatered. Wait for the soil to dry out before watering again.

Lily

Annual or perennial: Perennial

Latin name: *Lilium*

Family: Liliaceae

Growing zones: 4 to 9 for perennial; 3, 10, and 11 for annual

Growing season: Early summer to late fall

Start indoors or direct sow: Direct sow

Earliest planting: Fall, 4 weeks before the first frost

Sun needs: Full sun

Water needs: 1 inch of water weekly

Soil needs: Sandy loam

Suggested varieties for beginners: Tiger Lily, Stargazer, Casablanca

Yield per plant: Around 12 flowers

Troubleshooting tip: If planting in a lower or higher zone (3, 10, 11), plant your lilies in the spring rather than in the fall. Overwintering may not be as successful in less temperate zones.

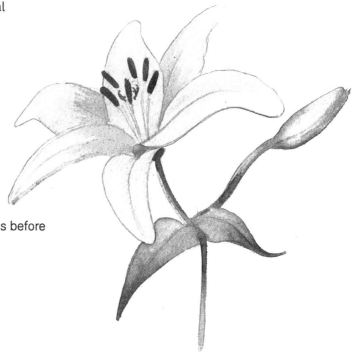

Snapshot

- Before you even see lilies in a garden, you smell their lovely perfume. The familiar, luscious scent fills any outdoor garden space, and the trumpet-shaped blooms are sure to impress. Coming in an array of colors including pink, orange, yellow, white, and red, lilies are a luxurious addition to your garden and make perfect focal flowers in arrangements. Be aware that all parts of the lily plant are poisonous, so be cautious planting around children and pets.

Starting

- Choose a location that receives 6 to 8 hours of sunlight. Lilies can be planted in the ground, beds, or containers, but be sure that the soil is 12 to 15 inches deep to allow ample room for root growth. Soil should be well-draining sandy loam.
- Use mulch around the base of the plant to keep in moisture, and amend the soil with a high-potassium fertilizer to encourage flower growth.
- Direct sow bulbs in the early fall, 4 weeks before the first frost. Plant bulbs three times as deep as the bulb is tall with the point facing up. Bulbs should be spaced 8 to 12 inches apart. Lilies look best when planted in clusters.

Growing

- Water lilies regularly to keep the soil slightly moist and the root system cool.

Harvesting

- Lilies produce one stem with multiple flowers on it. When harvesting, you can cut off the stem to use in arrangements or let it flower in the garden, removing any spent flowers as it ages. When cutting, be sure to only harvest the stem and allow the lower leaves of the plant to remain intact—these leaves will provide the bulb with nutrients if overwintering.

Overwintering

- When the plant has died back in the late fall, cut back all foliage. Apply a layer of mulch to protect it from the winter elements. Bulbs should be dug up every 3 years and divided.

Common Problems

- If your lilies are struggling with gray mold, make sure you are not watering them overhead, which adds excess moisture to the foliage. Also ensure that plants are spaced appropriately to allow for proper airflow.

Love-in-a-Mist

Annual or perennial: Annual

Latin name: *Nigella damascena*

Family: Ranunculaceae

Growing zones: 2 to 11

Growing season: Late spring to early fall

Start indoors or direct sow: Direct sow recommended

Earliest planting: Early spring or fall, if winters are mild

Sun needs: Full to partial sun

Water needs: 1 inch of water weekly

Soil needs: Nutrient-rich, sandy loam

Suggested varieties for beginners: Albion Green Pod, Cramer's Plum, Miss Jekyll Dark Blue

Yield per plant: Cut and come again

Fun fact: Love-in-a-mist is named for the airy spikes of foliage that appear around the blossom, creating a "mist" effect.

Snapshot

- This unique flower is stunning at every stage of growth. With their dainty foliage, fluffy flowers, and textural seed pods, love-in-a-mist make beautiful cut flowers and filler in arrangements. They can be found in a true blue, white, and some purples, adding cool, earthy tones to your garden.

Starting

- Love-in-a-mist does best in locations that receive full sun, but it will also grow in partial afternoon shade. Choose a location where soil is loamy and well-draining.
- Direct sow seeds in the early spring, planting 9 inches apart and barely covering the seed with soil, because they need light to germinate. Keep the soil moist during germination.

- Love-in-a-mist does not like being transplanted; however, if necessary, it can be started indoors 4 to 6 weeks before the final frost. Plant outside after the last frost.

Growing

- Water the plant two to three times weekly, keeping the soil moist but not wet. Use 1 inch of water weekly, unless there is a dry spell, in which case adjust as needed.
- Use a neutral fertilizer around the time of active growth to encourage more blooms. Plants are usually low and wide and do not need staking or corralling.

Harvesting and Drying

- When picking fresh flowers, cut when they are just beginning to open. If cutting for dried flowers, cut when the seed pod has developed and is firm.
- The seed pods make for a special texture in dried arrangements. Cut when the seed pods are fully developed and hang upside down in a cool, dry location for 2 weeks.

Seed Saving

- Love-in-a-mist will easily reseed itself if not cut or deadheaded. To collect seeds, wait for the pods to fully form on the plant and dry. Pods can be harvested, and seeds can be taken out and stored until planting.

Common Problems

- Love-in-a-mist will go to seed quickly and is a more short-lived flower. To keep plants blooming to the fall, succession plant your seeds every few weeks.

Nasturtium

Annual or perennial: Annual

Latin name: *Tropaeolum majus*

Family: Tropaeolaceae

Growing zones: 2 to 11

Growing season: Late spring to early fall

Start indoors or direct sow: Direct sow recommended

Earliest planting: 1 to 2 weeks after last frost

Sun needs: Full sun to partial shade

Water needs: Keep the soil moist but not overly wet

Soil needs: Well-draining

Suggested varieties for beginners: Jewel Mix, Alaska Mix

Yield per plant: Cut and come again

Keep in mind tip: Nasturtiums are trailing or climbing plants, depending on the variety. When adding nasturtium to floral arrangements, use them as wispy elements that can trail low in the arrangement.

Snapshot

- These classic garden staples cheer up any space with their bright jewel-toned blossoms and whimsical vines. Nasturtiums are simple to grow and abundant throughout the summer months. Their shell-like shape adds a playful element to floral design, and they can even be added to salads, as both the flowers and leaves are edible.

Starting

- Nasturtiums thrive in pots, planters, raised beds, and directly in the ground. Find a location that gets full to partial sun and has well-draining soil. In warmer climates, nasturtiums do well with afternoon shade.
- Direct sow seeds after the last frost. Space seeds 8 inches apart and cover with ½ inch of soil. Keep the soil moist during germination.

- Although nasturtiums are sensitive to having their roots disturbed, they can be started indoors 3 to 4 weeks before the last frost, if desired, and planted outside after hardening off after the final frost.

Growing

- During the growing season, keep the soil moist but not wet. To avoid mildew or fungal problems, water at ground level instead of overhead.
- Different varieties of nasturtiums require different supports. Some nasturtium varieties are climbers and will need a trellis. Some are trailing and can be planted in a hanging planter or allowed to trail along the ground.

Harvesting

- Harvest nasturtium blossoms as they are just beginning to open. Clip down low to get a long stem, if using the foliage for floral design. If harvesting the plant to eat, flowers can be picked when they are in full bloom.

Seed Saving

- Nasturtiums readily self-seed. If you want to contain the plant, it is best to grow them in a planter. Seeds are large and can be harvested from the seed pods after they dry out completely on the plant.

Common Problems

- Nasturtiums are prone to aphid infestations and are often used as "sacrificial" plants in vegetable gardens to attract aphids before they get to the other plants. To avoid aphids, pinch off any affected stems as soon as you see them. You can also purchase ladybugs from your local feed store to release onto the infected plants.

Phlox

Annual or perennial:
Annual

Latin name: *Phlox drummondii*

Family: Polemoniaceae

Growing zones: 4 to 8, but depends on variety

Growing season: Summer to first frost

Start indoors or direct sow: Direct sow recommended

Earliest planting: As soon as soil can be worked in the early spring

Sun needs: Full sun

Water needs: Keep the soil moist, but do not overwater

Soil needs: Rich, sandy loam

Suggested varieties for beginners: Cherry Caramel, Leopoldii, Sugar Stars

Yield per plant: Cut and come again

Keep in mind tip: The annual flower phlox is slightly different from garden phlox. For one, garden phlox is a perennial and grows much taller and bushier than annual phlox. However, annual phlox is the more common variety in cut flower gardening, flower farming, and flower arranging.

Snapshot

- This petite filler flower is an unsung hero of the cut flower garden. Phlox produces ample blooms throughout the season in an array of colors, adding depth to your garden and arrangements. Flowers range from pinks, purples, creams, whites, and reds, and they bloom in clusters of star-shaped petals.

Starting

- Phlox does best in full sun to partial afternoon shade. Choose a location with well-draining soil that gets 6 hours of sunlight.
- Plant after the last frost. Seeds should be directly sown 8 to 12 inches apart and covered with ⅛ inch of lightweight soil.
- Phlox don't like root disturbance, but they can be started indoors and transplanted outside, if desired. Start seeds 4 to 6 weeks before the final frost and transplant outdoors afterward.

Growing

- Keep the soil moist by watering low. Phlox greatly benefits from an irrigation drip line.
- When growing phlox, stabilize them by creating a grid with plastic netting. To do this, place stakes in every corner of your garden bed. Lay netting across the bed and tie it halfway up your stakes to create a hovering grid. Phlox will grow through it.

Harvesting

- Cut when half of the flowers on the stem are open. Cut stems down low and at stem junctions.

Seed Saving

- To harvest seeds from garden phlox, allow the flowers to die back and dry on the plant; small seed pods will form where the blossoms were. Pinch off the seed pods and store in a cool, dry location until ready to be planted the following season. Seed collecting from annual phlox is more challenging than with garden phlox, and it is often easiest to purchase new seed packets yearly.

Common Problems

- The most common problems phlox face are powdery mildew, aphids, and going to seed too quickly. To prevent powdery mildew, avoid overhead watering and overcrowding plants. Aphids can be remedied by introducing ladybugs into the environment or clipping back affected plants. Deadhead and cut often to prevent plants from going to seed too soon.

Rose

Annual or perennial: Perennial

Latin name: *Rosa*

Family: Rosaceae

Growing zones: 4 to 11, depending on the variety

Growing season: Late spring to early fall

Start indoors or direct sow: Purchase bare roots or potted plants and transplant

Earliest planting: Early spring for cooler zones, fall for temperate/warmer zones

Sun needs: Full sun

Water needs: Thorough, deep watering two or three times per week

Soil needs: Sandy loam, pH of 5 to 7

Suggested varieties for beginners: Lady of Shalott, Desdemona, Peace

Yield per plant: Varies with age and variety

Keep in mind tip: Growing roses is a time investment! Although newly planted bare-root roses can and do flower in their first season, it may take years for a rose bush to become a dependable cut flower. Be patient, and your investment will pay off.

Snapshot

- This is the queen of the flower garden. Roses have long been a favorite of gardeners and provide romance and elegance in arrangements. Roses come in a wide variety of colors, shapes, and sizes, so be sure to research what varieties do best in your region before planting.

Starting

- Choose a location that receives at least 6 hours of sunlight. Morning sun and some afternoon shade is the best combination. Soil should be sandy loam, well-mulched to retain moisture, and well-draining enough to prevent standing water.
- Roses should be purchased as bare roots or established plants. Bare roots are a cut-back version of the plant, not yet rooted in soil. These can easily be ordered from reputable rose shops, such as David Austin. When planting bare-root roses, soak for 8 to 12 hours in a bucket of water prior to planting. Then dig a large hole, amend with compost, and transplant.
- If planting a potted rose, gently loosen the roots before planting. Plant your rose and mound up soil and mulch around it. Water thoroughly.

Growing

- Water deeply two or three times per week. Do not overwater.
- During the blooming season, fertilize roses monthly with an organic rose fertilizer, such as a 4-8-4 blend.

Harvesting

- Deadhead roses weekly by cutting off the spent bloom all the way back to the next leaf set below it, where the plant will send new growth.
- When harvesting, always cut back to a leaf set. For the best results, use pruners instead of garden scissors.

Overwintering

- Cut off all dead branches, but do not do a hard prune (where the entire plant is cut back). Generously mulch around the base of the rose plant, and water when weather gets dry in fall and winter.

Common Problems

- Roses can be susceptible to black spots, a common fungal disease. To prevent this, avoid overhead watering and keep foliage dry. To treat, use a nontoxic fungicide. A common gardener hack for halting black spots is to mix 1 tablespoon of baking soda with 1 gallon of water and spray the mixture on leaves.

Scabiosa

Annual or perennial: Perennial

Latin name: *Scabiosa caucasica*

Family: Caprifoliaceae

Growing zones: 3 to 7

Growing season: Summer to fall

Start indoors or direct sow: Start indoors

Earliest planting: 6 to 8 weeks before the last frost

Sun needs: Full sun

Water needs: 1 inch of water weekly

Soil needs: Well-draining, slightly alkaline

Suggested varieties for beginners: Fama Deep Blue, Salmon Rose, Black Knight

Yield per plant: Cut and come again

Keep in mind tip: When grown as a perennial, scabiosas can be divided every 2 to 3 years to multiply your number of plants. When dividing your plant, do so at the beginning of the season in spring. Separate your plant into multiple clusters and then plant.

Snapshot

- Scabiosas are one of the most giving plants you could grow in your garden. They bloom profusely throughout the season with flowers in shades of blue, pink, white, and red. These interesting blooms resemble pincushions, resulting in their common name, "pincushion flower." Their blooms and seed pods make for fun, sought-after textures in flower arrangements.

Starting

- Start seeds indoors in seed cell trays 6 to 8 weeks before the final frost. Barely cover the seedlings with soil or vermiculite.
- Harden off after the last frost and plant outside 12 to 15 inches apart. Scabiosas do well in raised beds with well-draining soil. Choose a location that

receives 6 to 8 hours of sunlight. In warmer climates, scabiosas benefit from afternoon shade.
- When plants are around 8 inches tall, pinch back the center stem to promote lateral growth and more stems.

Growing
- Scabiosas like moist soil during active growing. Once mature, plants should receive 1 inch of water weekly.
- Stabilize scabiosas by creating a grid with plastic netting. To do this, place stakes in every corner of your garden bed. Lay netting across the bed and tie it halfway up your stakes to create a hovering grid. Scabiosas will grow through it.

Harvesting and Drying
- Scabiosas bloom quickly and need to be harvested regularly. Cut blooms when they are in their "pincushion" stage, before the petals have fully opened.
- Harvest scabiosa pods when they are dry on the plant.

Seed Saving
- Let the flowers form seed pods on the plant, and collect the pods when they are fully dried out. Store in a cool, dry location until ready to plant the following spring.

Common Problems
- Scabiosas are susceptible to powdery mildew. To avoid, make sure not to overhead water them, which can add extra moisture to the foliage. Instead, water at the base of the plant or use a drip line. In addition, be sure that plants are spaced to allow for proper airflow.

Snapdragon

Annual or perennial: Annual

Latin name: *Antirrhinum majus*

Family: Plantaginaceae

Growing zones: 3 to 11

Growing season: Spring to fall

Start indoors or direct sow: Start indoors

Earliest planting: 8 to 10 weeks before the last frost

Sun needs: Full sun to partial shade

Water needs: 1 inch of water weekly

Soil needs: Rich, well-draining soil

Suggested varieties for beginners: Rocket Mix, Madame Butterfly Mix

Yield per plant: Multiple stems

Troubleshooting tip: In growing zones 7 and up, snapdragons can be grown as a short-lived perennial. However, if your growing zone is too cold, don't worry; snapdragons can be grown as an annual everywhere.

Snapshot

- These flowers send up colorful spires that attract an array of pollinators. Snapdragons are aptly named for their resemblance to a dragon's face; when gently pressed on either side, the petals will open and close like a dragon's mouth. Their stems grow multiple smaller blossoms that open from the bottom to the top.

Starting

- Grow snapdragons in full sun to partial shade. Plant in soil that is rich in nutrients, well-draining, and has a pH of 6 to 7.
- Seeds should be started indoors 8 to 10 weeks before the last frost. Light is required for the seeds to germinate, so do not cover the seeds. Once the final frost has passed, harden off seedlings and plant outdoors. Space seedlings 5 to 10 inches apart.

- Snapdragons can be found at local nurseries, but be careful: Many snapdragon plants are intended for landscaping and will have short stems. Grow snapdragons from seed if the intended use is for arrangements.

Growing
- Water 1 inch weekly. Avoid overhead watering.
- Stabilize snapdragons by creating a grid with plastic netting while growing. To do this, place stakes in every corner of your garden bed. Lay netting across the bed and tie it halfway up your stakes to create a hovering grid. Snapdragons will grow through it.

Harvesting
- Harvest when one-third of the flowers are open. When harvested at this stage, snapdragons will live just over a week in a vase.

Seed Saving
- Allow the flowers to go to seed on the plant, becoming small pods. Pluck the seed pods off the plant, puncture the pod, and pour seeds into a paper envelope or container. Store seeds in a cool, dry location until next season.

Common Problems
- Rust is a common fungal infection caused by damp foliage on snapdragons. To avoid, water plants at ground level or use a drip irrigation system. Also be sure to use correct spacing between plants to encourage airflow.

Stock

Annual or perennial: Annual

Latin name: *Matthiola incana*

Family: Brassicaceae

Growing zones: 7 to 10

Growing season: Late spring to
late summer

Start indoors or direct sow: Sow indoors

Earliest planting: 5 to 6 weeks before the
last frost

Sun needs: Full sun to partial shade

Water needs: 1 inch of water weekly

Soil needs: Rich, well-draining soil

Suggested varieties for beginners:
Antique Pink, Iron Series, Katz Series

Yield per plant: 1 to 3 blooms

Fun fact: According to the traditional
Victorian *language of flowers,* gifting
stock as a cut flower demonstrates
adoration and affection. Different colors can also mean different
things—white, for example, represents
happiness and contentment.

Snapshot

- Stock blooms are fluffy, romantic
  flowers that emit a sweet floral smell.
  They are a staple in English cottage gardens and are also known by the name
  "gillyflower." Commonly found in pinks, purples, and whites, stock has been
  hybridized into gorgeous, subtle tones like antique peach and mauve. They are
  a favorite in gardens and arrangements alike.

Starting

- Start seeds indoors 5 to 6 weeks before the final frost in composted, well-draining soil. Seeds should be sown ¼ inch deep and will germinate in 1 to 2 weeks.
- Harden off seedlings after the last frost and plant outside, ideally in raised beds that get morning sun and afternoon shade. Seedlings should be spaced 6 to 9 inches apart.

Growing

- Stock should be watered consistently when the temperatures rise; do not over-water. Avoid powdery mildew by watering at the base of the plant rather than overhead.
- Deadhead stock to encourage more stems to bloom.

Harvesting and Drying

- Harvest stock when one-third to one-half of the blossoms have bloomed on the plant. Stems should be cut down to a leaf set.
- Stock can be dried. Simply hang cut stock upside down in a cool, dry location for 2 weeks until the flowers have dried out thoroughly.

Seed Saving

- After the flowers have completely finished blooming and dried on the plant, seed pods will form. Carefully remove the seed pods from the plant, then empty their seeds into a paper envelope or jar. Save for the following season.

Common Problems

- Stock can be susceptible to overwatering and aphids. Check your plants daily for stunted growth and proper water levels in the soil. If aphids are spotted, cut off affected stems. Live ladybugs can also be introduced to feed on aphids.

Yarrow

Annual or perennial: Perennial

Latin name: *Achillea millefolium*

Family: Asteraceae

Growing zones: 2 to 9

Growing season: Early summer to early fall

Start indoors or direct sow: Start indoors

Earliest planting: 8 to 10 weeks before the final frost

Sun needs: Full sun

Water needs: 1 inch of water weekly

Soil needs: Sandy loam

Suggested varieties for beginners: Summer Pastels, Paprika, Apple Blossom

Yield per plant: Cut and come again

Keep in mind tip: Yarrow can be commonly found at nurseries. If purchasing a preestablished plant, plant it in the fall. If starting from seed, start indoors in the late winter to early spring.

Snapshot

- This organic, wild-looking plant features a collection of tiny blooms at the top of a long, stalky stem. Yarrow plants have feathery foliage with stems that shoot up three to four times as tall as the plant itself. Coming in shades of pink, white, red, yellow, peach, and orange, it makes a great filler flower in arrangements.

Starting

- Start yarrow seeds indoors 8 to 10 weeks before the final frost date. Seeds need light to germinate, so do not cover with soil.
- Harden off seedlings after the last frost.
- Once acclimated, plant yarrow outdoors, ideally in raised beds or in-ground. Yarrow can grow in containers, but they need well-draining, well-composted soil. Select a location that receives at least 6 hours of sunlight and plant seedlings 1 to 2 feet apart.

Growing

- Maintaining yarrow is relatively simple. Plants need 1 inch of water weekly but are drought-tolerant.
- Plants may need staking or corralling if they grow too large. To corral, stake the corners of your flower bed and tie twine in between to keep plants upright.

Harvesting and Drying

- Harvest yarrow when the daily temperature is the lowest. Yarrow can easily wilt if cut during the midday heat. Wait until flowers are open enough to see the pollen.
- Yarrow is a wonderful dried flower. Hang stems upside down in a cool, dry location for 2 weeks and flowers will retain their shape and color.

Seed Saving

- Wait until flowers are fully dry and brown on the plant. Cut off dried stems and position flowers over a jar or bag. Gently brush the top of the dried flowers with your thumb to scrape the seeds out into the container. Save in a cool, dry location until next season.

Common Problems

- Is your yarrow plant flopping over? It could be that it needs more water, or it could be that it needs deadheading. Because yarrow plants can grow tall stems, it is important to deadhead regularly. This will reduce the amount of weight up top and encourage the plant to send out new growth.

Zinnia

Annual or perennial: Annual

Latin name: *Zinnia elegans*

Family: Asteraceae

Growing zones: 2 to 11

Growing season: Summer and fall

Start indoors or direct sow: Start indoors or direct sow

Earliest planting: 4 weeks before the final frost date

Sun needs: Full sun

Water needs: Water when the soil is dry (drought-tolerant)

Soil needs: Well-draining

Suggested varieties for beginners: Queen Lime, Giant Salmon Rose, Oklahoma Series

Yield per plant: Cut and come again

Keep in mind tip: Zinnias benefit greatly from being pinched back early in the season. Once plants are 8 to 10 inches tall, gently cut the center stem back by around 4 inches to an established leaf set. This will encourage your zinnia plant to branch, which will in turn provide you with more blooms!

Snapshot

- If you only grow one flower in your first year of cut flower gardening, this is it. Zinnias have colorful, sturdy, cheerful blossoms that bloom throughout the summer and into the fall. They are one of the easiest flowers to grow and will produce ample blooms throughout the season.

Starting

- Zinnias germinate and grow quickly and can be started inside or direct sown. If starting indoors, sow seeds 4 weeks before the last frost. Harden off and plant after the final frost.
- If direct sowing, choose a location—container, raised bed (preferred), or in-ground—with full sun and well-draining soil. Plant seeds after the final frost and cover with ¼ inch of soil, spaced between 8 and 10 inches apart.
- Plant starters can be bought from local nurseries. However, be aware that many of these plants are not intended as cut flowers and will not produce long stems.

Growing

- Zinnias are drought-tolerant and should be watered when the soil starts to become dry to the touch. Water at ground level.
- Large plants may need to be corralled to prevent them from falling over.

Harvesting

- To harvest zinnias, do a "wobble test." Pinch the stem gently about 6 inches down from a flower and wiggle it. If the flower head wobbles on the stem, it isn't ready. If the stem is firm, it is ready to be cut.

Seed Saving

- To save zinnia seeds, wait until the flowers are fully dry and brown on the plant. Gently pinch the center of the dried flowers to pull out seeds and transfer into a container. Save in a cool, dry location until next season.

Common Problems

- Zinnias encounter few problems throughout the season. However, they can be susceptible to powdery mildew if overwatered or overcrowded. To avoid, be sure to water plants at ground level and space appropriately.

DAHLIA [page 146]

9

Fall Flowers

Amaranth

Annual or perennial: Annual

Latin name: *Amaranthus*

Family: Amaranthaceae

Growing zones: 2 to 11

Growing season: Summer to fall

Start indoors or direct sow: Start indoors recommended

Earliest planting: 4 to 6 weeks before the final frost

Sun needs: Full sun

Water needs: 1 inch of water weekly

Soil needs: Well-draining

Suggested varieties for beginners: Hot Biscuits, Red Spike, Coral Fountain

Yield per plant: Multiple blooms

Fun fact: Amaranth was, and continues to be, grown as a grain. Because of this, flowering amaranth can also be dried and fed to chickens as a high-protein food!

Snapshot

- With cascading blooms of red, orange, and green, amaranth is a showstopper in the cut flower garden. The flowering stems can grow upright or trail, depending on the variety. Plants have rich-colored leaves and make uniquely textural cut flowers, or can be dried and preserved.

Starting

- Start seeds indoors 4 to 6 weeks before the final frost date. Harden off seedlings after the final frost. Transplant seedlings outdoors in a raised bed or in-ground garden with full sun. (If growing in a warm climate, amaranth may benefit from some afternoon shade). Use well-draining soil and space seedlings 12 to 15 inches apart.

- If desired, seeds can also be directly sown in the garden once the final frost has passed. When planting, barely cover the seeds with a light dusting of soil.

Growing

- Plants need 1 inch of water weekly. To avoid powdery mildew, be sure not to overhead water.
- Some varieties of amaranth grow to be 6 to 10 feet tall! Stake plants as needed to provide support.

Harvesting and Drying

- Harvest amaranth flowers when the blooms are three-quarters of the way developed. When kept in clean water, stems will last around a week.
- Dry amaranth by hanging it upside down in a dark, dry location for 2 weeks.

Seed Saving

- To harvest seeds in the fall, let the amaranth flowers fully open and dry on the plant. Find a container such as a jar or a paper envelope, place it under the blooms, and gently rub the seeds off the flower into the container. You will be left with seeds and seed husks. To separate them, gently blow on the seeds and the husks will fly away.

Common Problems

- Are your amaranth plants becoming leggy? Amaranth can be sensitive to too much nitrogen in the soil. To fix this, amend the soil with a mulch containing fine wood chips, which will draw out excess nitrogen.

Aster

Annual or perennial: Depends on variety

Latin name: *Aster*

Family: Asteraceae

Growing zones: 3 to 8

Growing season: Late summer to fall

Start indoors or direct sow: Start indoors recommended

Earliest planting: 6 to 8 weeks before the final frost date

Sun needs: Full sun

Water needs: Keep the soil moist, but not sopping wet

Soil needs: Sandy loam with a pH of 5 to 7

Suggested varieties for beginners: Tower Series

Yield per plant: Varies by variety

Keep in mind tip: Asters come in many varieties that have different specifications for growing. Many common-variety asters are bushy, daisylike garden perennials. However, China asters are more common in cut flower gardens, and they are grown as annuals.

Snapshot

- These classic fall flowers come in a large array of shapes, sizes, and colors, and bloom just as the summer flowers are slowing down. Asters are known for their daisylike appearance, but the hybrid China aster is more ruffled and layered, reminiscent of a dahlia or peony. Asters have a fantastic vase life, making them a favorite cut flower among gardeners.

Starting

- Start seeds indoors 6 to 8 weeks before the final frost date. Harden off seedlings after the final frost, then plant them in in-ground gardens, raised beds, or containers. Choose a location with full sun and well-draining soil. Plant seedlings 6 to 12 inches apart.

- If desired, seeds can also be directly sown in the garden once the final frost has passed. Sow seeds about 1 inch deep.
- Aster plants can be purchased from the nursery; however, keep in mind that these asters tend to be shorter and bushier and are meant more for landscaping than cutting.

Growing

- Soil should be kept moist to the touch, but not so wet that it drowns the roots. Water 1 inch weekly.
- Asters can benefit from monthly fertilizing. Choose a well-balanced fertilizer meant for flowers, and stop fertilizing at the end of the summer.

Harvesting and Drying

- Asters should be cut just as the petals are beginning to open. Place immediately in cool, fresh water. When used as a cut flower, asters can last upward of 10 days.
- Asters make fabulous dried flowers! When the blooms are fully open, hang to dry in a cool, dark location for 2 weeks.

Seed Saving

- To save aster seeds, let the flowers go to seed and form fluffy seed pods reminiscent of dandelions. To harvest, pull off the fluffy chaffs and find the seed attached at the bottom. Seed can be stored in a cool, dry location until ready to be planted next season.

Common Problems

- If you notice stunted growth on your plants and the yellowing of leaves, your asters may have "aster yellows" disease, which is spread by leafhoppers. To deter this infection, make sure to clear out all debris and clipped foliage in your garden space. To solve this problem, affected plants need to be removed to stop the spread.

Celosia

Annual or perennial: Annual

Latin name: *Celosia*

Family: Amaranthaceae

Growing zones: 6 to 11

Growing season: Summer to fall

Start indoors or direct sow: Start indoors

Earliest planting: 6 to 8 weeks before the final frost

Sun needs: Full sun

Water needs: 1 inch of water weekly

Soil needs: Rich, well-draining soil

Suggested varieties for beginners: Flamingo Feather, Pampas Plume, Chief Mix

Yield per plant: Cut and come again

Troubleshooting tip: Celosias (also called cockscombs) do not tolerate cold temperatures. If you want to keep your celosia plant as a perennial but cannot overwinter it, try planting it in a container and bringing it indoors for the season. Just be sure to provide it with ample light!

Snapshot

- Celosia is one of the most distinctive flower varieties that grows in a cut flower garden. With their array of colors, mixtures of textures, and surprising shapes, these fall blooms make a wonderful addition to fresh and dried arrangements. Celosias put off lots of paintbrush- or coral-like blooms, and they continue to flower up until the frost.

Starting

- Start seeds indoors 6 to 8 weeks before the final frost date. Seeds need light to germinate, so do not cover with soil.
- After the final frost, harden off seedlings and plant outdoors in raised beds, containers, or in-ground. Celosias grow well in all locations so long as the soil is well-draining, and they receive full sun. Space the plants 12 to 18 inches apart.

Growing

- Plants need 1 inch of water weekly. Be sure not to overhead water to avoid powdery mildew.
- Celosias can grow quite tall—be sure to pinch your seedlings when they are around 8 inches in height to promote lateral growth.

Harvesting and Drying

- Celosias are unique in that the blooms continue to enlarge until they go to seed. Cut whenever they reach your desired size.
- Celosias can be dried by hanging them upside down in a dark, dry location for 2 weeks. Flowers will keep their color and are beautiful in dried arrangements or wreaths.

Seed Saving

- Let the celosia flowers fully open and dry on the plant. Find a container such as a jar or a paper envelope, place it under the blooms, and gently rub the seeds off the flower into it. You will be left with seeds and seed husks. To separate them, gently blow on the seeds and the husks will fly away.

Common Problems

- Celosias do not contend with many problems; however, plants can get overgrown or go to seed quickly. To avoid stalky plants, be sure to deadhead and harvest regularly.

Dahlia

Annual or perennial: Annual

Latin name: *Dahlia*

Family: Asteraceae

Growing zones: 3 to 11; 7 and below for annual, 8 and up for perennial

Growing season: Late summer to the first frost

Start indoors or direct sow: Direct sow

Earliest planting: Late May to early June

Sun needs: Full sun

Water needs: Keep the soil moist, but not waterlogged

Soil needs: Rich, well-draining

Suggested varieties for beginners: Cornel Bronze, Linda's Baby, Jowey Winnie, Café au Lait

Yield per plant: Cut and come again

Keep in mind tip: Dahlias grow from tubers that multiply every year. Tubers can be dug up annually and divided to increase your number of plants. They can also be overwintered in the ground, but remember to dig at least every other year to divide.

Snapshot

- With thousands of different varieties in almost every color, it's not hard to see why dahlias are a favorite among many cut flower gardeners. Plants range from 3 to 6 feet in height and put off flowers throughout the growing season.

Their unique shapes and sizes make them stand out—with their Anemone, Ball, and Dinnerplate varieties, you'd be hard-pressed to find a more versatile flower.

Starting

- Dahlias can thrive in many different garden locations, including raised beds and containers. Plant them in full sun with composted and well-draining soil.
- Tubers should be planted outside from May to June. Space tubers 12 inches apart, and plant them 6 inches deep with the eye (where the sprout forms) pointing up.

Growing

- Do not water dahlias until the sprouts are aboveground and a few inches tall, because the tubers are susceptible to rot. Once sprouted, soil should be kept moist but not oversaturated.
- Be sure to pinch your dahlia seedlings when they are around 8 inches tall to promote lateral growth, and stake them as they grow to add support.

Harvesting

- Dahlias do not continue to bloom once cut, so harvest when blooms are three-quarters of the way open.

Seed Saving

- Though dahlias are usually grown from tubers, their seeds can also be harvested and planted. To collect seeds, wait until the flower has fully opened on the plant, exposing a seed pod. Wait for that to turn brown and dry out, then pinch off the seeds.
- To collect tubers, dig up the tuber clumps, wash, let dry, and store in a cool, dry location for the winter. Divide tubers before planting in the spring. Find more resources on how to divide tubers in the back of this book (page 160).

Common Problems

- Dahlias can attract slugs. To keep them away, treat the ground around your plants with Sluggo Plus, which is pet- and child-safe and will discourage slugs from feasting on your leaves.

Marigold

Annual or perennial: Annual

Latin name: *Tagetes*

Family: Asteraceae

Growing zones: 2 to 11

Growing season: Summer to fall

Start indoors or direct sow: Start indoors recommended

Earliest planting: 4 to 6 weeks before the final frost

Sun needs: Full sun

Water needs: 1 inch of water weekly

Soil needs: Sandy loam with a pH of 6 to 7

Suggested varieties for beginners: African

Yield per plant: Cut and come again

Fun fact: Marigold flowers are often used as a natural pigment and can dye fabrics a beautiful deep orange or yellow. To extract the dye, boil the flowers for 30 minutes, then soak the fabric for 45 minutes or until your ideal color is achieved.

Snapshot

- Did you know that marigolds can act as a natural repellent? They can protect your garden from mosquitoes, deer, and rabbits. These cheerful, ruffly pom flowers are an easy-to-grow addition to your cut flower garden. Although marigolds are best known for their vibrant orange blooms, hybrids in white, yellow, and cream hues add variety to arrangements. Some varieties of marigolds are on the shorter side, but African marigolds are tall and simple to care for.

Starting

- Start seeds indoors 4 to 6 weeks before the final frost date.
- Harden off seedlings after the final frost and plant outdoors in an in-ground garden, raised bed, or container. Choose a location that receives full sun and has well-draining soil, and space seedlings 12 to 18 inches apart.

- If desired, seeds can also be directly sown in the garden once the final frost has passed.
- Marigolds can also be purchased from the nursery; however, keep in mind that these plants tend to be shorter and bushier, and are meant more for landscaping than cut flowers.

Growing

- Keep the soil well-watered without oversaturating it during the active growing season. Once plants are established, they will be more drought-resistant, but still benefit from 1 inch of water weekly.
- Marigolds benefit from regular cutting and deadheading to prevent them from going to seed and encouraging the plant to produce more blooms.

Harvesting and Drying

- Harvest when the flowers are almost all open but the centers are still tight. Strip the stems of foliage before placing in cool, clean water.
- Marigolds make wonderful dried flowers and will keep their color. Hang cut stems in a dry, dark location for 2 weeks to fully dry out the blooms.

Seed Saving

- Wait for the flower to die and dry on the plant. Gently pluck off the seed pods and pull the seeds out. Store in a cool, dry location for the following season.

Common Problems

- With their compact shape and ample foliage, marigolds can easily become susceptible to powdery mildew if watered overhead. Water plants at base level or install a drip irrigation system for best results.

Mum

Annual or perennial: Annual (for cut flowers)/perennial

Latin name: *Chrysanthemum*

Family: Asteraceae

Growing zones: 5 to 9

Growing season: Late summer to fall frost

Start indoors or direct sow: Start indoors recommended

Earliest planting: 6 to 8 weeks before the final frost

Sun needs: Full sun

Water needs: 1 inch during active growing, 2 inches during blooming

Soil needs: Rich, well-draining

Suggested varieties for beginners: Candid, Mocha, Coral Charm, Moira

Yield per plant: Cut and come again

Keep in mind tip: Starting chrysanthemums from seed can be exciting, because you never know what you're going to get. Mum seeds are never an exact replica of the plant, so you may not know what the blooms will look like until it flowers. Buy rooted cuttings of chrysanthemums to get a specific variety.

Snapshot

- Chrysanthemums are quintessential fall flowers. Their wide array of colors and exceptionally long vase life make them a favorite of florists and cut flower gardeners. Mums also bloom in many different forms—from daisylike blossoms to spiky spider mums to large, ruffled football mums, there is something for everyone!

Starting

- Start seeds indoors 6 to 8 weeks before the final frost date.
- Harden off seedlings after the final frost and plant outdoors in an in-ground garden, raised bed, or container. Choose a location that receives full sun and has well-draining soil, and space seedlings 18 to 24 inches apart.
- If desired, seeds can also be directly sown in the garden once the final frost has passed.

- Mums can also be purchased from the nursery. Buying plant starters directly from a garden center or flower farm can be a reliable way of growing a certain variety.

Growing
- Soil should be kept moist to the touch; water 1 inch weekly until the weather starts to cool, and then reduce.
- Choose a well-balanced fertilizer that is high in nitrogen and potassium to encourage blooming. Fertilize once at the beginning of the growing season.

Harvesting
- Harvest mums when flowers are almost fully open but the centers are still tight. Strip the stems of foliage, and flowers can last upwards of 10 to 14 days in clean water.

Seed Saving and Overwintering
- In zones 5 to 9, mums can be grown as a perennial, lasting for three or four seasons. After the frost has killed the foliage, cut back the leaves and stems, leaving a short amount aboveground. Cover the plant with mulch and do not water over the winter.
- Collect seeds by letting the flower dry on the plant. Seeds will form in the center of the spent blooms and can be harvested by gently pulling them out and storing.

Common Problems
- Mums can often attract earwigs, which will munch on their leaves or petals. Spray plants with water to dislodge pests when spotted.

Rudbeckia

Annual or perennial: Annual

Latin name: *Rudbeckia hirta*

Family: Asteraceae

Growing zones: 3 to 9

Growing season: Late summer to fall

Start indoors or direct sow: Start indoors

Earliest planting: 5 to 7 weeks before the final frost

Sun needs: Full sun

Water needs: 1 to 2 inches of water weekly

Soil needs: Well-draining, tolerates low-quality

Suggested varieties for beginners: Sahara, Indian Summer, Cherry Brandy

Yield per plant: Cut and come again

Troubleshooting tip: If your rudbeckias seem to be putting off fewer flowers during the season, be sure that you are keeping up on deadheading. This plant will start to slow flower production if they are not being cut, so harvest away!

Snapshot

- Commonly called "black-eyed susans," rudbeckia flowers are recognizable by their warm-toned petals and dark centers. As part of the daisy family, rudbeckias often have one to three layers of petals that come in yellows, reds, oranges, and browns. These flowers bloom on top of long, sturdy stems, making them perfect for fall flower arrangements.

Starting

- Start seeds indoors 5 to 7 weeks before the final frost date. Light is required for germination, so barely cover with a dusting of soil.
- Harden off seedlings when multiple sets of leaves form and the frost has passed.

- Plant in a location with full sun to partial afternoon shade and well-draining, moist, composted soil. Space seedlings 12 to 18 inches apart.

Growing

- Rudbeckias do not need constant watering and should be watered only when the surrounding soil feels dry to the touch. They do not need to be fertilized during the growing season.

Harvesting and Drying

- Harvest blooms as they are just starting to open. Flowers will fully open in water and will last about 10 days as a cut flower.
- Although the petals of rudbeckia tend to shrivel during the drying process, the center cones of the flowers add an earthy texture to dried arrangements and wreaths.

Seed Saving

- Once the flower heads and stems are dried on the plant, the seeds are ready to be harvested. Cut off the dried flower heads and place in a large container with a lid. Shake the container to dislodge the seeds and chaffs. Pour the seeds and chaffs through a kitchen strainer to take out some of the bigger chaffs. Gently blow on the mix to encourage the remaining chaffs to fly away, leaving the seed behind, ready to be stored.

Common Problems

- Rudbeckias can suffer from gray mold if watered overhead. Be sure to water plants at the base and to space them appropriately to allow for proper airflow.

Strawflower

Annual or perennial: Annual

Latin name: *Xerochrysum bracteatum*

Family: Asteraceae

Growing zones: 3 to 11

Growing season: Midsummer to the first hard or "killing" frost

Start indoors or direct sow: Start indoors recommended

Earliest planting: 4 to 6 weeks before the final frost

Sun needs: Full sun

Water needs: 1 inch of water weekly

Soil needs: Sandy loam

Suggested varieties for beginners: Apricot Mix, Vintage White, Copper Red

Yield per plant: Cut and come again

Keep in mind tip: When starting seeds indoors, strawflower needs light to germinate, so do not cover the seeds. The seeds are also very small; to ensure they don't wash away while watering, water from the bottom and allow the soil to soak it upward.

Snapshot

- Commonly known as "everlasting flowers," strawflowers add a fanciful, papery texture to the cut flower garden. They earned their nickname due to their thin, dryish petals. In fact, when dried, their petals remain almost the same as when alive: bursting with color, accented by a yellowish orange center.

Starting

- Start seeds indoors 4 to 6 weeks before the final frost date.
- Harden off seedlings after the final frost and plant outdoors in an in-ground garden or raised bed with well-draining soil. Choose a location that receives full sun and space seedlings 10 to 12 inches apart.
- If desired, seeds can also be directly sown in the garden once the final frost has passed in regions that experience warmer temperatures.

Growing:

- Although plants are fairly drought-tolerant, water 1 inch weekly if it hasn't rained. To avoid powdery mildew, be sure not to overhead water.
- Strawflowers can grow tall; to add support, stake or corral them as they grow.

Harvesting and Drying

- Strawflowers open and close daily with the sun and temperatures; in the early morning, you'll find them closed, but by the end of the day they could be fully open! Pick in the early morning and place in water immediately.
- Strawflowers are often grown just to be dried! Hang stems to dry upside down in a dark, dry location for 2 weeks.

Seed Saving

- Allow the flowers and stems to turn brown and dry on the plant. The center of the spent flowers will become fluffy, and the seeds and chaffs can be pulled out. Separate the chaffs from the seeds, and store in a cool, dry location until the following season.

Common Problems

- Strawflowers generally do not have many problems but may become affected by "aster yellows" disease, which is spread by leafhoppers. To identify, look for yellowing leaves and stunted growth. To deter, make sure to clean up all debris in your garden, as it attracts leafhoppers. Affected plants need to be removed to stop the spread.

Sunflower

Annual or perennial: Annual

Latin name: *Helianthus*

Family: Asteraceae

Growing zones: 2 to 11

Growing season: Summer to fall

Start indoors or direct sow: Direct sow recommended

Earliest planting: After the final frost

Sun needs: Full sun

Water needs: 1 inch of water weekly

Soil needs: Sandy loam

Suggested varieties for beginners: ProCut Series

Yield per plant: Up to 20 blooms

Troubleshooting tip: If your plant is growing exceptionally tall but it blooms infrequently or has oddly shaped flowers, you may have an excess of nitrogen in the soil. Conduct a soil test and amend with mulch.

Snapshot

- The classic look of yellow sunflower blooms in a late-summer garden patch is one that many gardeners look forward to each year. This quintessential fall flower can bloom in yellows, whites, burgundies, browns, and even with hints of blush. Sunflowers are known for growing tall stems and producing large flowers—sometimes larger than a dinner plate!

Starting

- Sunflowers should be planted in full sun. The plants are heliotropic, meaning that the flower heads will follow the sun. Planting in full sun will encourage the plant to grow straight instead of leaning over for light.

- Direct sow seeds after the last frost. Plant the seeds 1 to 2 inches deep with 4 to 6 inches between seedlings. The closer sunflowers are planted, the smaller the plants will grow.
- If desired, seeds can be started indoors 2 to 3 weeks before planting outside after the final frost.

Growing

- Plants need a medium amount of water: 1 inch of water weekly. To avoid powdery mildew, be sure not to overhead water.
- Some varieties of sunflowers can grow to be 8 feet tall! Be sure to pinch your sunflower seedlings when they are around 8 inches tall to promote lateral growth, and stake them as they grow to add support.

Harvesting

- Cut sunflowers just as the color is starting to show as they open. Although this may seem early, the flowers will continue to bloom after cutting and will have a longer vase life.

Seed Saving

- To save sunflower seeds, let the flower die on the plant. Harvest the blooms, leaving about a foot of stalk, then hang-dry the stalks for a few more days. Once fully dry, place the flower heads over a container and gently rub the flower center to dislodge the seeds and chaffs. Separate the chaffs from the seeds, by adding seed and chaff to a bowl and shaking until the chaff pieces rise to the top. Store in a cool, dry location.

Common Problems

- Sunflower seeds are a favorite snack of birds and rodents alike. To deter them from munching your blooms, cover the flower buds with netting or a large organza bag, which will protect the flower while allowing it to grow till harvest.

RANUNCULUS [page 96]

Zone Map

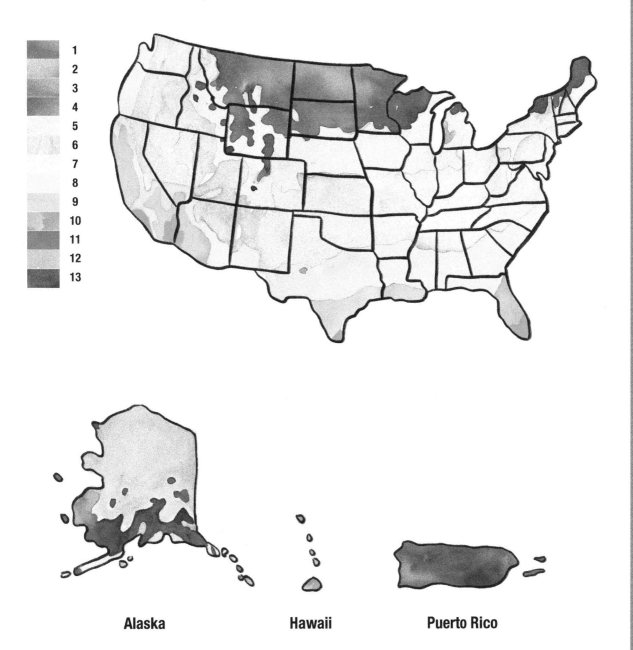

1
2
3
4
5
6
7
8
9
10
11
12
13

Alaska   Hawaii   Puerto Rico

Resources

Bulb and Corm Suppliers
Brent and Becky's Bulbs: BrentAndBeckysBulbs.com
Longfield Gardens: Longfield-Gardens.com

Create Your Own Compost Pile
The Old Farmer's Almanac: Almanac.com/how-compost-guide-composting-home

Dahlia Tuber Dividing
Summer Dreams Farm: SummerDreamsFarm.com/dahlia-tuber-and
-splitting-guide

Dahlia Tuber Suppliers
River Merle Farm: RiverMerleFarm.com/shop?page=2
The Farmhouse Flower Farm: TheFarmHouseFlowerFarm.com

Drip Irrigation
DripWorks: DripWorks.com

Gardening Tools
Johnny's Seeds Tools and Supplies: JohnnySeeds.com/tools-supplies

More Gardening Techniques and Information
Raven, Sarah. *A Year Full of Flowers: Gardening for All Seasons*. Bloomsbury, 2021

Regional Average Frost Dates
The Old Farmer's Almanac: Almanac.com/gardening/frostdates

Rose Bare-Root Suppliers
David Austin Roses: DavidAustinRoses.com/pages/shop-online

Seed Suppliers
Floret Flowers: Shop.FloretFlowers.com/collections/seeds
Johnny's Seeds: JohnnySeeds.com/flowers

Soil Testing Labs by State

Gardening Products Review: GardeningProductsReview.com/state-by-state
-list-soil-testing-labs-cooperative-extension-offices

References

"13 Common Garden Weeds." Almanac.com, February 9, 2022. almanac.com /content/common-garden-weeds.

Floret Flowers. "Seeds A–Z." shop.floretflowers.com/collections/seeds-in-stock.

Floret Flowers. "Soil Preparation." April 10, 2019. floretflowers.com/soil -preparation/?utm_source=pinterest&utm_medium=social.

Johnny's Seeds. "Flowers." johnnyseeds.com/flowers.

MasterClass. "How to Create Loam Soil for Your Garden." MasterClass. November 8, 2020. masterclass.com/articles/how-to-create-loam-soil-for-your-garden#what -is-loam.

McSheehy, Jill. *Vegetable Gardening for Beginners: A Simple Guide to Growing Vegetables at Home.* Emeryville, CA: Rockridge Press, 2021.

North Carolina Department of Agriculture & Consumer Services. "A Homeowner's Guide to Fertilizer." ncagr.gov/cyber/kidswrld/plant/label.htm.

The Old Farmer's Almanac. "Flower Growing Guides." almanac.com/plants /type/flower.

Raven, Sarah. *A Year Full of Flowers: Gardening for All Seasons.* New York: Bloomsbury, 2021.

The Spruce. "Plants A to Z." thespruce.com/plants-a-to-z-5116344.

Utah State University. "Gardener's Almanac Monthly Gardening Checklist." extension.usu.edu/yardandgarden/monthly-tips.

Index

Acknowledgments

To Nick: Your love and encouragement lift me up and motivate me to pursue my fullest potential for myself and our family. Thank you for your steadfast partnership and for doing all that you can to help me pursue my dreams.

To Van: Thank you for selflessly sharing your talents and passions with me to help showcase my love of flowers. Being your sister is such a gift.

To Mom and Dad: Thank you for instilling my passion for gardening, hard work, and pursuing my joys. You continue to be my biggest supporters, and I am forever grateful.

To Haley: Your friendship and flower knowledge are invaluable to me, and I wouldn't and couldn't be where I am today without you.

About the Author

Amy Barene lives in the Pacific Northwest where she runs her business, Capital Blooms. A self-taught cut flower gardener and florist, Amy combines her love of teaching with botanicals by empowering others to fill their yards with flowers. Capital Blooms was started in 2017 and consists of workshops, cut flowers, and floral arrangements as well as expansion into a cut flower garden podcast. Amy works on her 1,067-square-foot microflower farm with her husband, Nick, and three pups, Heidi, Cosmo, and Billie. When she isn't gardening, Amy loves hiking with her dogs, traveling, and finding the best cup of coffee in new towns. Keep up to date with Capital Blooms at CapitalBlooms.net.

CPSIA information can be obtained
at www.ICGtesting.com
Printed in the USA
JSHW021140090722
27916JS00003B/3

9 781685 391058